CONVERSATIONAL MARKETING

CONVERSATIONAL MARKETING

HOW THE WORLD'S FASTEST GROWING
COMPANIES USE CHATBOTS TO GENERATE
LEADS 24/7/365 (AND HOW YOU CAN TOO)

DAVID CANCEL
DAVE GERHARDT
EDITED BY ERIK DEVANEY

WILEY

For general information on our other products and services or for technical support, please contact our Customer Care Department within the United States at (800) 762–2974, outside the United States at (317) 572–3993 or fax (317) 572–4002.

Wiley publishes in a variety of print and electronic formats and by print-on-demand. Some material included with standard print versions of this book may not be included in e-books or in print-on-demand. If this book refers to media such as a CD or DVD that is not included in the version you purchased, you may download this material at http://booksupport.wiley.com. For more information about Wiley products, visit www.wiley.com.

Library of Congress Cataloging-in-Publication Data has been applied for and is on file with the Library of Congress.

ISBN 9781119541837 (Hardcover)
ISBN 9781119541868 (ePDF)
ISBN 9781119541899 (ePub)

Printed in the United States of America

V10006780_121018

Contents

Introduction: The Shift from Supply to Demand

Think about the way you buy products and services today compared to just 10 or 20 years ago. Whether you are buying a book (like this one), or renting a movie, or finding a ride to the airport, the buying experience has undergone a total transformation.

Today, instead of being forced to buy at a place and time that is convenient for *the company*, you can now buy just about anything from the comfort of your own home, or from your office, or from just about anywhere (provided you have an internet connection). And best of all, you can buy in real time or whenever is most convenient for *you*, the customer.

Today, Customers Have All the Power

Want to rewatch your favorite movie? Just a few years ago, that meant trudging to a video rental store and waiting in line so you could rent a DVD or VHS tape. Today, with just a few clicks, you can watch all of your favorite movies and TV shows on-demand—no waiting in line.

Ready to catch that ride to the airport? Just a few years ago, that meant walking to a cab stand, or trying to hail a cab from the sidewalk (not as easy as it sounds), or calling a cab company the day before, being put on hold, having to call back in the morning, and then never knowing for sure whether someone would show up. Today, you can schedule a ride on your phone with the push of a button and have it arrive at your door in a few minutes. (And you can track your driver's progress on a map inside the app so you know exactly when you'll be picked up.)

In this real-time, on-demand world we now live in, where access to an endless supply of products and services is always just a few clicks away, the marketers and salespeople vying for our business need to come to terms with a new, fundamental truth: The balance of power has shifted.

Today, customers have all the power. And the companies that end up winning in this new world will no longer be the ones that own the supply, but the ones that own the demand. Here are three key factors that led to this monumental shift.

1. Product Information Became Free

Gone are the days when companies could keep information about their products and services locked up and hidden away from their potential customers. Today, thanks to search engines, review websites, and social media recommendations, customers no longer need to rely on marketers or salespeople in order to educate themselves and make informed purchase decisions.

Instead of simply taking a company's word for it that their product or service is worth the price, or can solve a particular problem, today's buyers can consult a wide variety of resources and opinions in order to paint a fuller picture of what to expect from their purchase. And, of course, today's buyers aren't just researching and evaluating the potential benefits of the actual products; they are also evaluating the companies themselves and the level of service they provide, which leads me to factor number two:

2. Real-Time Interactions Became Expected

The second reason why customers have all of the power today: because real-time interactions have become the default. Today, billions of people around the world use real-time messaging for their day-to-day communication. More and more of us are chatting with our friends and family on messaging apps like WhatsApp, and at work we are chatting with our coworkers via messaging-powered collaboration tools like Slack.

As a result of this shift in how we communicate, coupled with the fact that we can now order so many products and services on-demand with just a few clicks, our customer expectations have evolved. We have become conditioned to expect real-time responses when we have questions and to expect instant solutions when we have problems.

3. Supply Became Infinite

Regardless of the product or service you are in the market for, today there are usually at least a handful of options you can choose from as a buyer. And in many cases, there are dozens of competitors all fighting for your dollars. (Just go to any supermarket and count how many different potato chip brands you see on the shelves.) As customers, that means we have more choice and can be more selective. As marketers and salespeople, it means that we can no longer expect our companies to win in a certain category just by "showing up" with our product—even if it's a good product. **Owning the supply isn't enough**.

Just look at the razor company Gillette, which dominated the razor industry for more than a century. Gillette's success stemmed from owning the design of their patented safety razor, owning the distribution centers for getting their razors out to retailers, and owning the relationships with those retailers. In other words, Gillette owned the supply. And for decades, if you wanted to buy a razor, you had no choice but to go to a brick-and-mortar retailer, like CVS or Walgreens, where you would inevitably find Gillette razors for sale on the shelves.

Then, in 2011, Dollar Shave Club appeared on the scene and turned Gillette's supply-driven model on its head. Instead of going head-to-head with Gillette and competing for shelf space, which was the approach competitors like Schick and BIC had taken, Dollar Shave Club went around the retailers and began selling their razors directly to consumers. To generate buzz for the new service, they crafted memorable marketing campaigns that stressed how expensive the razors in the stores were, how much of a pain it was to remember to buy them, and how all of the new features the supply-focused razor companies were adding to their products (like vibrating handles) were worthless. Then Dollar Shave Club presented their subscription service, which offered premium (but no-frills) blades at a lower price, as the solution. **Instead of focusing on owning the supply, they focused on owning the demand**.

In 2016, after years of sustained revenue growth, Dollar Shave Club was acquired by Unilever for a reported $1 billion. Over that same time period, 2011 through 2016, Gillette's North American market share dropped from 71 percent to 59 percent.

Winners and Losers: Why Companies Need to Adapt

For years, companies have been able to find success through creating amazing products and building loveable brands. But in a world of infinite supply, an amazing product and a loveable brand are no longer enough. In order to gain an advantage over the competition, you also need to provide incredible service. Those are the three moats you need to build around your business: product, brand, *and* service.

Today's customers care not only about *what* they're buying (product) and *who* they're buying it from (brand), but also *how* they're able to buy (service). They care about the buying process itself. And if that process takes too long, or feels too complicated, or doesn't meet their expectations, it's likely that those potential customers will go spend their money with a competitor.

Ultimately, Gillette was able to recognize that they needed to adapt to this fundamental shift in the way people prefer to buy. In 2017, they launched their own direct-to-consumer razor service, the aptly named Gillette On Demand. And while Gillette has (at least for now) been able to weather the storm brought on by Dollar Shave Club and other razor subscription services, not all supply-focused companies have been so fortunate.

Amazon vs. Borders

When Amazon first began selling books online in 1995, brick-and-mortar "superstores" dominated the industry. Borders, in particular, was generating around $1.6 billion in annual sales. At a time when there was a growing concern that super-stores like Borders would disrupt smaller, local bookshops, Amazon came along and pulled the rug out from under the entire industry. By 2006, Amazon had surpassed Borders in annual revenue (see Figure I.1), and by 2011, Borders, the former book retail juggernaut, was out of business.

Of course, the downfall of Borders cannot be solely attributed to the rise of Amazon, but it undoubtedly played a pivotal role. Amazon reinvented the way people buy books, and, with the launch of their Kindle e-reader in 2007, they also reinvented the way people read books. Before Amazon, book buyers had no choice but to go into brick-and-mortar

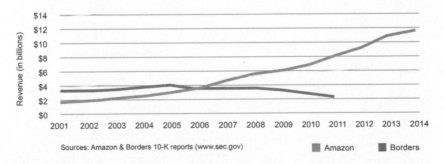

Sources: Amazon & Borders 10-K reports (www.sec.gov)　■ Amazon　■ Borders

FIGURE I.1 Tracking the rise of Amazon (and the decline of Borders) based on annual revenue growth.

stores, where they could find thousands of paperbacks and hardcovers lining the shelves. After Amazon, buyers could search through *millions* of titles online, and instead of having to fill up their own shelves at home with physical copies of books, buyers could have digital copies of books sent instantly to their e-readers.

While Borders did try to adapt to this new paradigm, they never fully embraced it. For example, in 2001, instead of launching their own online bookstore, Borders opted instead to outsource online sales to Amazon, a deal which lasted until 2007. And by the time Borders launched an e-book store in 2010 to compete with Amazon's Kindle Store, it was simply too little, too late. Today, Borders is no more, while Amazon (which is selling much more than just books these days) is valued at more than $800 billion.

Netflix vs. Blockbuster

When Netflix launched in 1997 with its video rental by mail service, Blockbuster was the undisputed king of the video rental industry. Between 1985 and 1992, Blockbuster grew from one location in Dallas to more than 2,800 locations around the world. In 1994, an acquisition by Viacom placed the company's value at $8.4 billion. Back then, no one could have predicted that by 2010, Blockbuster would be bankrupt...or that by 2011, Netflix would be pulling in more annual revenue than the once-undisputed king of the video rental industry (see Figure I.2).

Once again, we are looking at a case of a company failing to adapt to the new paradigm. As more and more customers began looking online to meet their video needs, first with rental by mail services, and then with on-demand streaming, Blockbuster stuck with the model they already knew. Instead of evolving the service they were providing in line with what customers wanted, they rested on the laurels of their well-known brand. And they banked on the fact that they owned the supply. By the time Blockbuster did catch on to how customer expectations were changing, launching

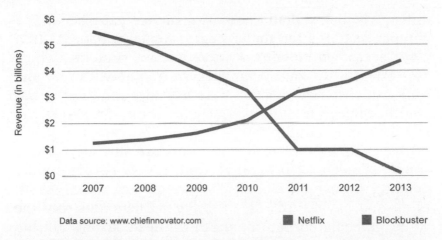

FIGURE I.2 Tracking the rise of Netflix (and the decline of Blockbuster) based on annual revenue growth.

their own Netflix-like service in 2004 and getting rid of late fees (which customers hated), it was too late. Netflix had already stolen the demand.

What makes this story especially poignant is the fact that, early on, Blockbuster had an opportunity to make an investment in the future of the company, but let it slip away. Back in 2000, Netflix CEO Reed Hastings reached out to Blockbuster and proposed a merger deal. Hastings wanted Blockbuster to acquire Netflix for $50 million, and as part of the deal, the Netflix team would manage Blockbuster's online brand. As you already know, that $50-million deal never happened—Blockbuster turned Hastings down. Today, Netflix is worth more than $150 billion.

Uber and Lyft vs. Yellow Cabs

For more than a century, taxicabs were the go-to mode of transportation for people trying to get from point A to point B without having to worry about finding parking or dealing with public transportation schedules. And they were painted yellow—a tradition started in 1908—to attract the attention of potential riders. But since the early 2010s, when Uber and Lyft launched their ridesharing services, traditional taxi companies have been under siege (see Figure I.3). In 2017, Uber surpassed New York City's yellow taxicabs (which are taxicabs that have been licensed by the city's Taxi and Limousine Commission) in trips per day, and the gap has continued to grow. Lyft has been gobbling up the yellow cab market share as well.

Even though taxicabs have historically owned the supply of rides, Uber and Lyft were able to generate more demand through offering easy-to-use apps that made scheduling and paying for rides a breeze. Customers saw the value immediately: no more struggling to hail a cab, no more counting out cash or having to fiddle with unreliable credit card machines. You just upload your payment information to the app once and you're ready to order rides on-demand.

In 2013, the cost of a New York City taxi medallion—the license required to operate a yellow taxicab—peaked at $1.3 million. By 2017, it had sunk to $241 thousand—one-fifth

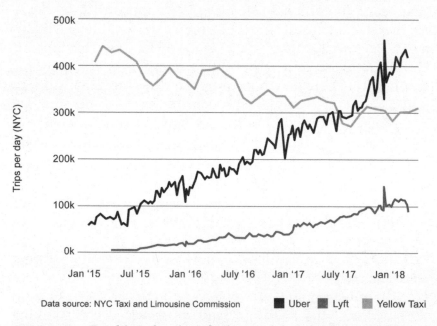

Data source: NYC Taxi and Limousine Commission   ■ Uber   ■ Lyft   ■ Yellow Taxi

FIGURE I.3   Tracking the rise of Uber and Lyft (and the decline of yellow cabs) in New York City based on trips per day.

of what it was worth just a few years before. Uber and Lyft (like Netflix and Amazon before them) have turned their industry on its head, and they did it by appealing to the preferences and expectations of their customers in order to create a superior customer experience. Both companies now have multi-billion-dollar valuations.

Why I Wrote This Book (and Why Now)

For the past two decades, I've been building software for marketing and sales teams, first at Compete, then at Lookery, then Performable, then HubSpot, and now at Drift. I've had thousands of conversations with marketers and salespeople from all around the world. I've gone into their offices and studied their habits and figured out what their pain points are. During this time period, I've watched as the balance of power has shifted from supply to demand, and from company to customer. I've watched as companies like Amazon, Netflix, and Uber have figured out how to deliver the real-time, on-demand buying experiences today's customers have come to crave. And finally, a few years back, it dawned on me:

The way we've been doing marketing and sales is broken. It was created for a world that no longer exists.

A visit to just about any business-to-business (B2B) or software as a service (SaaS) website will reveal the truth: Companies the world over are blatantly ignoring their potential customers. Instead of providing a real-time, on-demand buying experience for people who come to our websites and show interest in our products and services, we have been forcing people to fill out lead capture forms and wait for follow-up emails or phone calls. Instead of letting our customers buy when it is convenient *for them*, we've made it all about *us*. And we have become so obsessed with data and analytics and filling out spreadsheets and tracking every little detail that we have forgotten about *the people* we are serving.

The good news? The solution here is simple. In fact, it's been staring us in the face for centuries. As marketers and salespeople, we need to get back to basics. We need to return to the core of what the buying process has always been: **a conversation between buyer and seller**.

In your hands right now, you hold the playbook for harnessing the power of real-time conversations for your business: *Conversational Marketing*. Those new to the world of marketing and sales will come away with a step-by-step understanding of how you can start capturing, qualifying, and connecting with leads on your website through having real-time conversations. More experienced readers will gain a deeper understanding of how people prefer to buy in today's real-time, on-demand world, while also discovering new strategies and tactics that have been missing from the traditional marketing and sales playbook.

Today, more than 100,000 businesses are embracing the conversational marketing and sales methodology and adapting to the shift from supply to demand. But this is still just the beginning. I'm happy you are here to be a part of it.

David Cancel (@dcancel)

PART I

The Rise of Conversational Marketing and Sales

Chapter 1

Your Website Is Leaking Revenue (Here's How to Fix It)

Imagine seeing an advertisement for a new store that's just opened in your neighborhood, but when you walk into that store, there's no one there to greet you. In fact, there are no employees there at all. No salespeople walking the floor. No clerks behind the counters. And what makes the situation even more puzzling is that all of the store's shelves are empty. There are no actual products that you can sample or try out, only pictures and descriptions.

At first glance, this appears to be a store—a store that you just saw an advertisement for a few minutes ago, mind you—that won't let you buy anything.

But then you see it: Way in the back, there's an old, dusty table, and on that table is a pen and a clipboard. "Ready to buy?" the form on the clipboard says. "Just fill this out and we'll follow up with you later."

"But what if I'm ready to buy now?" you ask aloud to no one.

58% of B2B Websites Are "Empty Stores"...Is Yours One of Them?

The above scenario sounds ridiculous because it absolutely *is* ridiculous. No brick-and-mortar store would pay for ads and generate buzz only to ignore potential customers once they showed up. Unfortunately, that's exactly what most business-to-business (B2B) and software-as-a-service (SaaS) companies have been doing with their websites. According to eMarketer, B2B companies ended up spending a collective $4.6 billion on ads that drove people to their websites in 2018. Yet a majority of these companies are treating their websites like "empty stores."

Instead of greeting visitors when they drop by our websites, we've been ignoring them. Instead of offering visitors assistance in real time (while they're already right there and clearly interested), we've been making them fill out forms and wait. Worst of all, even when people *do* take the time to fill out forms, they're not guaranteed to get a response. In a study we did at Drift, which looked at the websites of 512 B2B companies, we found that 58% of companies never followed up with website visitors who filled out forms and tried to get in touch with sales.

By sticking to the old marketing and sales playbook (see Figure 1.1), we've been forcing potential customers into an overly complex buying process. It's a process that fails to acknowledge the fundamental shift that's happened in how people prefer to buy.

Today, half of all B2B customers expect a company's website to be helpful, while more than a third of customers expect a company's website to be the *most* helpful channel they use during the buying process, according to

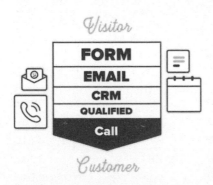

FIGURE 1.1 The old playbook for converting website visitors into customers.

research from BCG. So why are so many of us still treating our websites like empty stores? In doing so, we're letting potential customers (and potential revenue) slip through the cracks.

The Solution: Add Real-Time Messaging to Your Website

By adding a messaging or "live chat" tool to your website, you can start greeting your website visitors in real time when they drop by. You can let people know, up front, that your website is not just another empty store.

Setting up a simple welcome message that lets people know you're available to answer their questions is a great place to start. And best of all, it doesn't require a ton of work. (I've seen teams get up and running, and start having conversations, in less than five minutes.)

In addition to helping you provide a better buying experience on your website, so you can catch those leads who are slipping through the cracks, messaging offers another huge advantage for marketing and teams: It allows you to capture, qualify, and connect with leads *faster.* Here's why that's so important today. ....

90% of B2B Companies Don't Respond to Leads Fast Enough… Do You?

In a world of infinite supply, where customers have come to expect real-time responses as the default, companies no longer have the luxury of being able to make people wait. They can no longer control *when* a sale happens. Instead, marketing and sales teams need to be ready to help out at a moment's notice, as soon as someone has a question. Otherwise, that person might end up in the arms of a competitor.

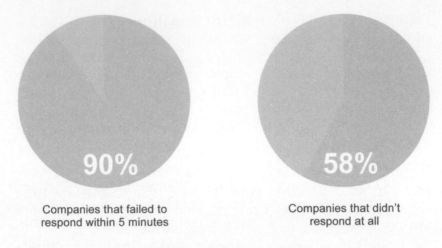

90%
Companies that failed to
respond within 5 minutes

58%
Companies that didn't
respond at all

Source: Drift 2018 Lead Response Report

FIGURE 1.2 Results from Drift's 2018 Lead Response Report.

A study from InsideSales.com, published in the *Harvard Business Review*, found that waiting five minutes to respond to a new lead resulted in a 10x drop in the likelihood of being able to connect and follow up with that lead. After ten minutes, there's a 400% drop in the odds of qualifying the lead. In other words, the longer you wait to respond after someone reaches out, the less likely it is that that person will convert. And for best results, companies should be staying below the five-minute mark.

Unfortunately, in the same Drift study where we looked at the 512 B2B companies, we found that 90% of companies failed to respond to sales inquiries within that five-minute sweet spot (see Figure 1.2).

This isn't too surprising when you take into account that just 15% of the companies we looked at were using real-time messaging on their websites. But even if you do use real-time messaging, there's no guarantee that you'll be able to respond to *every* lead within five minutes. After all, there are only so many hours in a day, and there are only so many employees available to respond to people. So, what do you?

The Solution: Use Artificial Intelligence to Provide 24/7 Service

There's been a lot of hype surrounding artificial intelligence (AI) and chatbots over the past few years. At one extreme, you have people who are worried that AI will take over the world—that intelligent machines will eventually come to replace humans in nearly every field and industry. At the other extreme, you have people who think intelligent machines are useless curiosities, and that they are more likely to distract and confuse potential customers than help them.

The truth, of course, lies somewhere in the middle. Our philosophy at Drift has been to use AI—specifically, intelligent chatbots—only for those tedious, repetitive tasks that AI is particularly well-suited for. The idea isn't to replace human marketers and salespeople, it's to supplement their efforts. And when it comes to responding to new leads as quickly as possible, 24/7, there's no denying the effectiveness of intelligent chatbots.

Without having to write a single line of code, marketers and salespeople can now add chatbots to their websites that can provide answers to common questions, route visitors to the right people and departments, ask qualifying questions, and schedule meetings for sales reps. By automating these tasks, chatbots enable marketers and salespeople to focus more of their time on tasks that require a human touch, like answering complex product questions and building rapport with new leads. So even though you're outsourcing some of the work to chatbots, the end result is a more human buying experience.

81% of Tech Buyers Don't Fill Out Forms . . . Are You Still Using Them?

One of the key reasons why today's B2B buying experience has become overly complex and unnecessarily slow is our reliance on lead capture forms. Pick up any book on B2B marketing and sales (excluding this one) and chances are there will be a section on setting up and optimizing lead capture forms and the landing pages they appear on. In fact, forms have become such an integral part of the traditional marketing and sales playbook that it can be hard for teams to even imagine how they could ever generate and qualify leads without them. (I know this first-hand because I watched my own marketing and sales teams go through it.)

For years, lead forms have been the engines powering our lead generation and lead qualification efforts. But today, the reality is that lead forms are no longer as effective as they once were. According to a survey conducted by LinkedIn, 81% of tech buyers don't fill out forms when they encounter gated content—they'd rather go look for that information elsewhere than go through the hassle of filling out a form. Bearing that in mind, it probably won't come as too much of a surprise to learn that the average conversion rate for landing pages these days is just 2.35%, according to Search Engine Land.

The underlying problem: While lead forms present a simple and scalable way for *companies* to capture and qualify leads, they completely ignore the preferences and expectations of *the customer.* By forcing buyers to share personal information in exchange for content and/or access to a sales rep's time, we're behaving as if there are no other resources or companies out there that those buyers can turn to (which obviously isn't the case). And by forcing buyers to wait for follow-ups, assuming we even take the time to follow up at all, we're ignoring the fact that today's buyers have come to expect real-time, on-demand responses when they engage with businesses.

Today, lead forms act as roadblocks in the buying process, slowing down sales cycles and putting a damper on customer experience. So why are so many of us still sticking to this "forms and follow-ups" approach? What alternative do we have?

The Solution: Replace Forms with Conversations

By using a combination of real-time messaging and chatbots on your website, you can easily replace lead capture forms with conversations. For example, while it's been common practice to add calls-to-action (CTAs) to the bottoms of blog posts that direct visitors to landing pages, where they can then fill out forms in order to download "premium" content (like ebooks or white papers), you can now create CTAs that initiate real-time conversations—either with actual people, if they're available, or with chatbots, which have your back when no one's around.

Best of all, when using conversations instead of forms, you don't need to send people away from the blog posts they're already reading, or the pages they're already on, in order to move them further down the sales funnel. Instead, you can engage with visitors wherever they are on your website. Whether it's a blog post, your homepage, your pricing page, or a "contact us" page, all you need to do is add a link that will trigger a real-time conversation.

Now, at this point, some of you might be thinking, "Wait…if I replace the forms on my website with conversations, how do I keep collecting all of the information I used to be collecting with forms? That's information my company needs." The answer is simple: You ask for it. The difference is that instead of learning about potential customers by forcing them to fill out static, impersonal lead forms, you can learn about them through having one-to-one conversations.

Even when it's a chatbot doing the talking, the experience is light years ahead of what you can provide with forms, and you end up learning more about potential customers than you would have otherwise. To quote management consultant Brad Power, writing for the *Harvard Business Review*: "This is the strength of an AI agent that can elicit information like a person, rather than an analytics tool that simply finds patterns in the data it collects, like a machine." (Power, 2017)

FIGURE 1.3 The old approach to converting website visitors versus the new approach.

The bottom line: By replacing lead forms with conversations, you're removing a roadblock from the buying process and replacing it with a fast lane for your best leads (see Figure 1.3).

Using Real-Time Conversations to Achieve Hypergrowth

Before the internet, before the telephone, before the printing press, businesses all over the world marketed and sold their products through having real-time, one-to-one conversations. And that's still how a lot of corner stores, mom and pop shops, and other small businesses market and sell today. But over time, businesses began to distance themselves from their customers.

As explained in the book *The Cluetrain Manifesto,* the rise of broadcast media and advertising broke down those personal connections and one-to-one conversations that had once driven marketing and sales: "For thousands of years, we knew exactly what markets were: conversations between people who sought out others who shared the same interests. Buyers had as much to say as sellers. They spoke directly to each other without the filter of media, the artifice of positioning statements, the arrogance of advertising, or the shading of public relations." (Levine, Locke, Searls, & Weinberger, 2000)

The future of marketing and sales will see businesses return to speaking directly to their customers and potential customers. As Joseph Jaffe, author of the book *Join the Conversation,* explained, the goal should be to have marketing and sales feel like a welcome guest, not an interloper. As Jaffe wrote on his blog: "There are literally millions of alive, flawed, human, passionate, influential and authentic conversations going on around you right now: isn't it time you joined in?...Through the power of community, dialogue, and partnership, marketing can be a conversation; a welcome guest in the homes, experiences and lives of our consumers." (Jaffe, 2010)

Today, nobody thinks of marketing and sales as a "welcome guest." And that's a direct result of the impersonal approach businesses have been taking for so long—an approach that values measurement and tracking and form-fills over creating an incredible buying experience. The good news: There's nothing preventing you from speaking directly with your customers and potential customers. And by doing so, you'll be able to unlock revenue that your business has been missing out on.

Early Results

By removing the roadblocks and hurdles that can get in the way of people talking to your business, you make it easier for people to buy. And that translates to a faster path to revenue.

At Drift, we've felt this faster path to revenue first-hand. Through abandoning the traditional marketing and sales playbook and embracing the power of conversations, we've seen our revenue grow by more than 10x compared to the first quarter of 2017. Drift has now become one of the fastest-growing B2B companies of all time, with our revenue growth exceeding the revenue growth that so-called "unicorn" companies including Salesforce, ServiceNow, Workday, and Zendesk experienced at the same stage in their company histories.

Since replacing our website forms with conversations, we've added 15% more leads to the top of our marketing and sales funnel. And to clarify, the leads we've generated through conversations haven't come at the expense of other leads sources (like product sign-ups or webinar sign-ups). Instead, these are net new leads—leads we would have otherwise been missing out on. Best of all, we're not just capturing more leads with conversations, we're capturing our best leads: Today, 51% of our business comes from the leads we capture through conversations.

Since making the switch to conversational marketing and sales, we've also seen the length of our sales cycle shrink drastically. According to a study from Implisit, which looked at the sales pipelines of hundreds of B2B companies, the average amount of time it takes for a lead to convert into an opportunity—that is, someone who has engaged with a sales rep and expressed into to buy—is 84 days. Meanwhile, at Drift, it takes an average of just three days for the leads we capture through conversations to book meetings with our sales reps. And we're not the only ones seeing these types of results.

For example, there's Richard Wood, who runs the Manchester, England–based marketing agency Six & Flow. Since adopting conversational marketing and sales, Wood has seen the length of his sales cycle drop by 33%. And then there's Andrew Racine, the former Director of Demand Generation at MongoDB, who grew opportunities by 170% after adding real-time conversations to the MongoDB website.

For Wood and Racine, using real-time conversations to drive growth didn't require a complete overhaul of their websites or marketing and sales software. Instead, by following the conversational marketing and sales methodology, they were able to quickly and easily plug conversations into what they were already doing.

The Conversational Marketing and Sales Methodology

Conversational marketing and sales is the process of having real-time, one-to-one conversations in order to capture, qualify, and connect with your best leads. Unlike traditional marketing and sales, it uses targeted, real-time messaging and intelligent chatbots instead of lead capture forms—that way leads never have to wait for follow-ups and can engage with your business when it's convenient *for them* (like when they're live on your website).

Of course, conversations with potential customers don't just happen on your website, which is why conversational marketing and sales is bigger than any single channel or platform. Combining inbound and outbound tactics, conversational marketing is all about starting a dialogue with the people who can benefit from what you're offering, whether that's via a face-to-face meeting, or a phone call, or an email exchange. Regardless of the medium, with conversational marketing you're not just blasting your messaging outward, or forcing people to take an action: You're answering people's questions, listening to their feedback, and then uncovering new ways to help them. In other words, you're having actual conversations.

Capture, Qualify, Connect

Look, I get it: Conversational marketing and sales can sound great in theory, but when it comes to actually putting it into practice, the details can become fuzzy. That's why at Drift we developed a methodology that shows you how to use conversations to turn visitors into leads, leads into opportunities, and opportunities into customers. We call it Capture, Qualify, Connect (see Figure 1.4).

FIGURE 1.4 An overview of the conversational marketing and sales methodology

Capture For the past decade, marketers have been pouring tons of time and energy into SEO and driving more traffic to their sites…only to make everyone fill out the same-old lead-capture form. With conversational marketing and sales, you replace the forms on your website with conversations. Specifically, you can use real-time messaging and/or an intelligent chatbot, both of which can be shown to specific visitors (or displayed on specific pages) based on the criteria you set.

If you're just starting out, we recommend letting your current website traffic determine where you surface your messaging widget or chatbot. Not getting much traffic? Put them everywhere so you can start as many conversations as possible. Lots of traffic? Target your high-intent pages only, like your pricing page—that way you can filter out some of the visitors who aren't serious about buying. You can even personalize your messages with a company's name or other information.

When a conversation starts, any contact information a lead enters (e.g. email, phone number) can be captured automatically. This is true whether it's a human doing the talking or one of your chatbots. And once contact information is captured, the conversation doesn't have to stop—a lead can continue on through your sales funnel at lightning speed, since all of their questions can be answered in real time.

Qualify By following the traditional marketing and sales playbook, companies would force their leads to wait days or weeks before the buying process could continue. With conversational marketing and sales, you can capture *and* qualify leads within minutes, which means you no longer have to worry about leads slipping through the cracks in your website.

In addition to having the humans on your team ask qualifying questions via real-time messaging, you can have chatbots ask the same qualifying questions when your team is offline. All you need to do is take the questions your team is already asking and turn them into a script for the chatbot. Here's a popular script framework we've seen companies using:

- Question 1: What brought you here?
- Question 2: Who are you? / What company do you represent?
- Question 3: How are you thinking about using our product?
- Call-to-action: Book a demo. / Get in touch with a human.

Granted, not everyone who goes through this qualifying script will make it to the final step. You control what the disqualifying criteria are. That way, when a chatbot hears a disqualifying answer, you can have it say something like, "Sorry, we don't think our product is a good fit for you at the moment." The leads who do qualify, meanwhile, can be routed automatically to the right sales rep (or the right sales rep's calendar).

Connect By setting up routing rules, you can ensure that the leads on your website always are connected to the right reps based on sales territory. And if you have multiple reps working in the same territory, leads can be assigned to reps on a rotating basis.

With some leads, however, you might need to give them a little nudge in order to get them back to your website. That's where email comes into play. Your sales reps can now send emails that include links for triggering real-time conversations. When a lead clicks that link, he or she is automatically connected to the sales rep who sent the email. But if that sales rep isn't available at that exact moment, it isn't a huge deal. Chatbots will always have your back and can hop in and keep the conversation going.

When it comes to setting up a time for a demo or meeting, leads can check the available times on a sales rep's calendar with the click of a button and then find the time that works best for them—and this all happens from within the same conversation window. A chatbot can then take care of sending out meeting invites to both sides. The end result is that your sales reps spend more time connecting with potential customers human-to-human and less time dealing with tedious tasks.

The Technology Powering the Transformation

Over the past several years, we've seen major paradigm shifts in almost every industry, from retail, to entertainment, to transportation. And wherever we look, whether it's Amazon versus Borders, Netflix versus Blockbuster, or Uber and Lyft versus taxicabs, the businesses that end up winning are the ones that focus on getting closer to their customers and delivering incredible experiences. Of course, there's no denying that the rise of the internet, streaming, and mobile technology helped make it possible for companies to deliver those types of experiences.

When wielded poorly, technology has the power to drive us apart. But when wielded intelligently, it can bring us closer together. When it comes to conversational marketing and sales, the rise of real-time messaging and intelligent chatbots have been instrumental to the creation of this new methodology—a methodology that puts the needs of the customer before the needs of the company.

In the next two chapters, we'll explore these two technologies, messaging and chatbots, more in-depth, and I'll explain how they should fit into your conversational marketing and sales strategy.

Chapter 2

The Rise of Messaging

A Real-Time Lead Generation Channel

Today, most business-to-business (B2B) and software-as-a-service (SaaS) companies rely on three main channels for communicating with their customers and potential customers:

1. Telephone
2. Email
3. Social media

For years, marketers and salespeople have been using these three channels to blast out their sales pitches, promotions, and other marketing messages. From cold calls to spam emails to never-ending streams of social media posts, the conversations on these channels have largely been one-sided. (In other words, they haven't really been conversations at all.)

As marketers and salespeople, it was easy for us to convince ourselves that those were the channels our customers were using, so those were the channels we needed to engage them on. And because the traditional marketing and sales playbook favors the obsessive measuring and monitoring of metrics like clicks and dials and email opens over providing an enjoyable buying experience, we justified all those interruptive phone calls we made and annoying "nurturing" emails we sent by saying that we had to hit our numbers. Back then, we valued being data-driven over being customer-driven. (Not that learning from the data you collect isn't important, it's just that what you learn directly from your customers, through talking to them one-on-one, is *more* important.)

After years of abusing these three channels—phone, email, and social media—and tapping them for all they were worth, marketers and salespeople have been slowly waking up to a new reality. It's a reality where buyers (including you and me) have grown sick of being bombarded with irrelevant and annoying phone calls, emails, and/or social media messages, and where we no longer rely on those three channels as our primary means of communication.

In this new reality, only 43% of people answer calls from unknown numbers (according to research from ThinkingPhones); the average email open rate for SaaS companies is just 21% (according to research from MailChimp); and, for the first time in its history, Facebook's user numbers have started to decline, especially among millennials. In 2017 alone, Facebook lost approximately 2.8 million of its U.S. users under the age of 25 (according to research from eMarketer), and the predictions for 2018 aren't looking any better.

Today, fewer and fewer people are using phone, email, and social media to communicate, and more and more of us—billions of us—are turning to real-time messaging. As marketers and salespeople, this is a fundamental shift we can't afford to ignore.

The Three Waves of Messaging (and How the Third Wave Changed Everything)

Whether it's a messaging app you use to talk to friends and family, or a collaboration tool you use to communicate with coworkers, real-time messaging has become the new engine

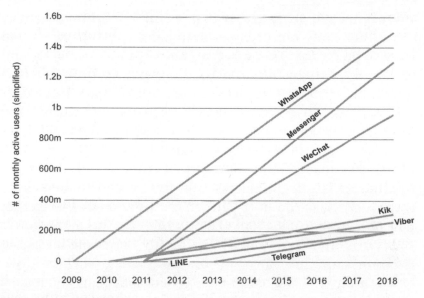

Data source: www.statista.com

FIGURE 2.1 The third wave of messaging has swept up billions of users.

that powers today's most popular communication systems. We are now living in what I call the third wave of messaging, and unlike the two waves that preceded it, this one has shown no signs of slowing down anytime soon (see Figure 2.1).

Over the past few years, the adoption and usage rates of messaging apps have skyrocketed. Today, the apps that make up this third-wave messaging don't have millions of users, they have *billions* of users. It was a shift that happened so rapidly that many marketing and salespeople didn't even notice it. And now we're all struggling to catch up.

Before we explore in-depth how this third wave of messaging is forcing us to rethink our marketing and sales strategy and to reimagine the way our customers buy from us, let's take a quick look back at how messaging technology has evolved over the past two decades.

The First Wave of Messaging

For many us, hearing the terms "messaging" and "instant messaging" might make us think of the age of dial-up internet; back when you had to listen to that awful screeching, staticky noise that came out of your computer's speakers when you tried to go online. This was the first wave of messaging, and it was kicked off by instant messaging services, including ICQ (launched in 1996), America Online (AOL) Instant Messenger (launched in 1997), Yahoo! Messenger (launched in 1998), and MSN Messenger (launched in 1999, rebranded as Windows Live Messenger in 2005, then discontinued in 2013 following Microsoft's acquisition of Skype in 2011).

One of the technologies this first wave of messaging introduced was the user-definable online co-user list, U.S. patent number US6750881B1, which is perhaps better known as the "buddy list." The buddy list made it easy to find and communicate with multiple friends in real time. It was a way to scale one-to-one conversations, and it attracted users by the millions. For example, while AOL Instant Messenger, also known as AIM, started out with just 900 simultaneous users on the night of its release, the service would later draw as many as 18 million simultaneous users (according to Mashable).

Within a few years, however, this first wave of messaging would begin to fizzle out as a new communication tool appeared on the scene: the affordable, mass-market cellular phone. (Remember Nokia's candy-bar-style phones? They were best-sellers in the late 1990s and early 2000s.) With the rise of the affordable cell phone came the rise of Short Message Service (SMS) text messaging, a technology that allowed phone owners to send short, real-time messages via cellular networks. According to the Pew Research Center, by 2005 there were 36 million monthly active SMS texters in the United States.

The Second Wave of Messaging

When using instant messaging services during the first wave, we had to sit at a computer in order to send and receive messages in real time. With the rise of SMS, we were able to access that same real-time messaging functionality from our cell phones. This was a game-changer, and it helped contribute to the dissolution of that first wave of messaging software.

For several years, SMS texting reigned as one of the most popular and most convenient channels for real-time communication. But it wasn't without its flaws, the most significant being its cost. Cellular service providers typically charge a fee based on the number of SMS texts users send and receive, which can lead to soaring cell phone bills (and unhappy customers).

Detecting an opportunity to disrupt SMS by offering a more affordable form of real-time communication for mobile devices, a handful of companies launched mobile messaging services in the mid-2000s. These services, which included Skype (launched in 2003), Blackberry Messenger (launched in 2005), and Google Talk (also launched in 2005, and now commonly known as Google Chat or Gchat), formed a distinct second wave of messaging.

And while this second wave of messaging knocked on SMS's door, so to speak, the third wave of messaging is actively breaking that door down.

The Third Wave of Messaging

The third wave of messaging, which kicked off in the late 2000s/early 2010s, makes the previous two waves seem like ripples. In this third wave, we're seeing messaging usage grow from hundreds of millions to billions of active users. And, in an example of history being cyclical, an evolution in phone technology is one of the root causes of this shift in how we communicate. Only in this case, instead of SMS disrupting messaging software, which was a result of the rise of affordable cell phones, we're seeing messaging software disrupt SMS, which is a result of the rise of affordable smartphones.

In the United States, the smartphone era began in earnest in 2007 with Apple's launch of the first iPhone. By 2013, more than half of U.S. adults (56%) owned a smartphone, and as of January 2018, that number has now climbed to 77%, according to the Pew Research Center.

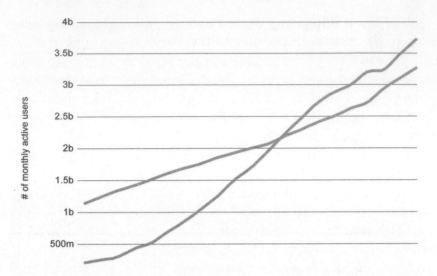

FIGURE 2.2 Messaging apps have become more widely used than social media.

With the rise of smartphones, of course, came the rise of mobile applications. And for the past several years, messaging apps have been among the most frequently down-loaded mobile apps. Messaging apps have also seen higher retention rates and usage rates compared to other types of apps, according to research from BI Intelligence. According to that same research, the world's four most popular messaging apps (WhatsApp, Facebook Messenger, WeChat, and Viber) now boast more active users than the world's four most popular social media sites (Facebook, Instagram, Twitter, and LinkedIn), and it's been that way since 2015 (see Figure 2.2).

When you look at the number of active users the messaging apps from this third wave are attracting (see Table 2.1), it becomes immediately obvious that messaging can no longer be characterized as some communication fad or fringe player: It's a communication revolution, and it's spreading around the world. Meanwhile, after peaking in 2014, revenues from SMS, as well as overall

TABLE 2.1	If WhatsApp were a country, it would be the most populous country in the world.	
Name of Messaging App	# of Monthly Active Users	Year launched
WhatsApp	1.5 billion	2009
Facebook Messenger	1.3 billion	2011
WeChat	980 million	2011
Kik	300 million	2010
Viber	260 million	2010
LINE	203 million	2011
Telegram	200 million	2013

SMS usage, have been in a steady decline (according to data from Portio Research).

But this shift isn't solely the result of more and more people using messaging, it's also the result of people choosing to use messaging more and more frequently over other channels. For 62% of mobile users between the ages of 30 and 44, messaging is now their preferred way to communicate with others, according to 2017 data from Statista. The same data shows that 61% of 18- to 29-year-olds share that preference, preferring to use messaging over voice calls or video calls. A 2016 report from App Annie, meanwhile, showed that mobile users aged 25 to 44 were spending nearly twice as much time using messaging apps compared to email apps. Mobile users aged 13 to 24 were spending eight times as much time using messaging apps compared to email apps.

As marketers and salespeople, the sheer number of people flocking to messaging apps should be enough to get our attention. After all, in order to truly understand our potential customers, we need to understand how they prefer to communicate with each other on a day-to-day basis. But here's the thing: People today don't just want to use messaging to talk to each other. They also want to use it to talk to businesses.

Why 90% of Global Consumers Want to Use Messaging to Talk to Businesses

In the 1990s, back during the first wave of messaging, companies began to offer messaging-based customer support on their websites. Known as "live chat" or "online chat," these services left a lot to be desired. While theoretically allowing for real-time communication between customers and companies, these messaging services were often slow and clunky, and, in many cases, customers would still end up needing to make a phone call (or send an email or submit a support ticket) before being able to resolve their issues. What's more, customers rarely knew *who* they were actually talking to when reaching out via live chat. To customers, these representatives or "chat agents" were nameless, faceless corporate entities, and the overall customer experience they provided wasn't exactly being raved about.

Over the years, however, messaging technology has improved. And the rise of mobile has made being able to communicate with companies via messaging more desirable among today's buyers. A 2009 study from Bold Software, for example, found that 63% of online buyers who used a website's chat feature reported being more likely to return to that website, while 62% reported being more likely buy from that website again. More than a third of buyers (38%) said that the chat session itself had been the reason they had decided to buy. Then there was a 2010 study from Forrester, which showed that 44% of online buyers believe having questions answered by a live person during a purchase is one of the most important features a website can provide. One of the conclusions Forrester drew from that study was that using messaging proactively could help companies achieve multiple business goals, including increasing customer satisfaction, improving conversion rates, and reducing churn.

Flash forward to 2013: Econsultancy publishes a study showing that 73% of people who used a website chat feature for customer support had a positive experience, making messaging the most popular customer support channel. Email came in second place, with 61% of people reporting a positive experience, then apps (53%), social media (48%), and phone (44%). A study published by BoldChat a year earlier helps explain why messaging has become such a dominant channel for customer communication. The study found that people who prefer talking to businesses via messaging—or live chat, as they refer to it here—do so for several reasons, but the most common one is the ability to have questions answered immediately (see Table 2.2). Specifically, 79% of respondents agreed that receiving real-time responses was one of live chat's standout features. Forty-six percent of respondents, meanwhile, agreed that live chat was the most efficient mode of communication.

By 2016, 90% of global consumers expected to be able to talk to businesses via messaging, according to a study from Twilio. That same study found that 66% of people preferred using messaging for talking to businesses over any other communication channel. For more and more customers, messaging is becoming their preferred way of

TABLE 2.2	**Why do people prefer to use live chat for talking to businesses?**
Reason for preferring live chat	**Percent of respondents who agreed**
My questions answered immediately	79%
Because I can multitask	51%
It's the most efficient communication method	46%
Once I used live chat I realized how well it works	38%
Better information than if I emailed	29%
Because I'm in control of the conversation	29%
I don't like talking on the phone	22%
Because I can chat while I'm at work	21%
Better information than if I called	15%

communicating with businesses. As a marketer or salesperson, when you consider this evolution in how customers prefer to communicate, it begs the question: Why have we only been using messaging for customer support, and not for marketing and sales as well?

The Rise of Messaging for Marketing and Sales

When I launched the first iteration of the Drift conversational marketing and sales platform in 2016, most of the B2B world still only saw messaging as a customer support tool. But within a few days of using messaging to engage with visitors on the Drift website, including potential customers, the value of using messaging for marketing and sales became apparent.

By adding messaging to your website, you're not only opening up a new communication channel, but you're also opening up a new lead generation channel. And the leads you generate from messaging aren't siphoned off from another source. As we've seen first-hand at Drift, adding messaging to your website yields you net new leads (which means if you don't have messaging on your website, chances are you're currently letting leads slip through the cracks). Best of all, messaging is a real-time lead generation channel, which means marketing and sales teams can capture and qualify leads faster than ever before, and buyers no longer have to wait.

Instead of powering marketing and sales with lead forms and follow-ups, thanks to the rise of messaging you can now power marketing and sales with real-time conversations. And based on a 2017 study of thousands of B2B websites, conducted by Drift in partnership with Clearbit, we found that people from all over the world are flocking to websites and seeking out a real-time buying experience. Specifically, we found that the people visiting business websites, starting conversations, and converting into leads were coming from every single country (all 195 of them). In addition to every country being represented in the data, every business sector was represented as well (see Figure 2.3). This illustrates just

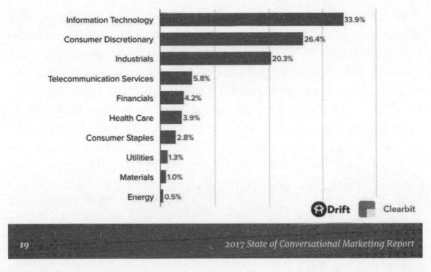

FIGURE 2.3 Buyers from every sector are using messaging to start sales conversations.

how broad the appeal of being able to communicate with businesses via messaging has become.

Today, making messaging part of your marketing and sales strategy isn't just a smart move, it's the only move. Because if you fail to adapt to the way your customers prefer to communicate, those customers will inevitably leave you for a competitor who does adapt.

Remember: whoever gets closest to the customer wins.

Using Messaging to Capture and Qualify Leads in a Single Step

By following the old marketing and sales playbook, we have inadvertently been putting distance between ourselves and our potential customers. And it's our use of lead forms, as well as our reliance on outdated communication channels, that are largely to blame. When you force someone to fill out a lead form, you are effectively putting up a stop sign. (Or, more specifically, you are putting up a sign that says:

"We can't be bothered to talk to you right now, but if you hand over a bunch of personal information, we'll follow up later . . . assuming you're a good fit for our product.")

Instead of engaging with website visitors and figuring out whether they're a good fit right then and there, while they're live on our websites, we've been waiting hours, days, or even weeks to follow up . . . assuming we follow up at all. For years, we've been treating capturing leads and qualifying leads as two distinct functions. That's led to both a poor experience for buyers, as they have to wait for a response before they can buy, as well as longer sales cycles for marketing and sales teams.

The good news: By adding messaging to your website, you can eliminate the time gap between when you capture leads and when you qualify them. And that's because with messaging, you can capture *and* qualify a lead during a single conversation. There's no magic or painstaking work required—it just comes down to being helpful, asking the right questions, and treating the person you're talking to like an actual person, and not like an entry in a customer relationship management (CRM) system.

The Importance of Treating Leads Like People

When you use a lead form to learn about someone on your website, you're not acknowledging the person's presence in that moment. You're effectively ignoring him or her, which helps explain why conversion rates for lead capture forms are so low. More and more people are becoming less and less willing to give away information about themselves just because some form on a website demands it.

When you use messaging to learn about someone on your website, on the other hand, the dynamic completely changes. Instead of showing that website visitor a stop sign, with messaging you're opening up an E-Z Pass or FasTrak lane and waving that visitor on through. Instead of collecting information by forcing that visitor to fill out a form, you're collecting that same information through having a real-time conversation. And you'll notice that after you've talked to someone for a few minutes, after you've listened to his or her concerns and answered his or her questions and offered advice, asking for an email address and for information about his or her company suddenly doesn't feel like such a big ask.

By having a real-time conversation via messaging, you're able to learn about potential customers in a more natural way, right away. You can figure out right then and there, during a single conversation, whether or not someone is going to be a good fit for your product or service. And as soon as that person enters an email address, he or she can automatically be saved in your system as a new contact. It all happens right there in a messaging window, no follow-up emails or phone calls required.

But . . . How Does It Scale?

One of the most common pieces of pushback I hear when I talk about using messaging for marketing and sales is scalability. To some, the idea of talking to hundreds or thousands of website visitors and trying to identify the ones who would be a good fit to buy might sound impossible (or if not impossible, like a huge misuse of resources). But when you actually begin to use messaging on your website, a few things immediately come to light.

First, as a real-time communication channel, messaging is inherently more scalable than making phone calls. Instead of the "smile and dial" approach to sales outreach, which requires going down a list and talking to people one at a time, with messaging you can talk to multiple leads simultaneously. That's why using messaging to answer customer questions has historically cost around half as much as using a call center, according to 2012 research from Telus International. A single marketer or salesperson using messaging can do the work of four, five, or six marketers or salespeople using phones.

The second thing you'll notice about using messaging to communicate with website visitors at scale: You can easily filter incoming conversations so your sales reps, business development reps (BDRs), and/or sales development reps (SDRs) aren't stuck talking to people who are never going to buy. For example, if you're a B2B company that only sells to companies based in a specific country or geographic region, you can set up messaging so only people from those target areas can see it. It's the same deal if you only sell to companies of a certain size: You can set targeting conditions so only people from those types of companies will see a messaging widget and/or welcome message on your website. By setting up routing rules and creating separate inboxes for Sales and Support, you can also make sure your reps aren't tied up talking to existing customers and answering support questions. With messaging, it's easy for your marketing and sales team to hone in on just those visitors who are likely to buy.

Depending on how much website traffic your company is generating, however, you may need employees from other teams to step up and join conversations. In the early days at Drift, back when we only had a few dozen employees, the entire company was responsible for managing the conversations happening on our website. We broke each day of the week into shifts and divided those shifts among all employees. It didn't matter whether you were an engineer, a marketer, a support person, or a sales rep—at least once a week, you were talking to customers and potential customers one-to-one via messaging. Not only did scheduling these shifts help make messaging more scalable, but it also helped bring our employees closer to our customers.

Of course, at some point employees need to go home and sleep, and go on vacation, which means running a real-time lead generation channel on your website around the clock may inevitably become impossible . . . unless you have backup.

In Chapter Three, we'll explore how chatbots are helping companies deliver conversational marketing and sales at scale, 24 hours a day, seven days a week.

Chapter 3

The Rise of Chatbots

Personal Concierges for Your Website Visitors

Picture this: It's Sunday, 2 a.m., and all of your company's marketers and sales reps are sound asleep, dreaming about meeting (and exceeding) their lead generation and revenue goals.

Meanwhile, halfway across the country, an executive from a billion-dollar firm is on your company's website. She starts on the homepage but eventually navigates to your company's pricing page, where she spends several minutes reading about the different product plans you offer.

Then she leaves your website. She doesn't fill out a form, she doesn't interact with anyone at your company, and when your marketers and salespeople go into the office on Monday morning, they have no clue that an executive from a billion-dollar firm had even been on your company's website, let alone on the pricing page.

Now, picture this slightly different scenario. It's the same setup: Sunday, 2 a.m., your marketers and sales reps are snug in their beds, and that same executive is on your website again, checking out your pricing page. Only this time, before she leaves, she sees a message pop up in the corner of the screen:

HereToHelpBot: "Hey there! Thanks for stopping by. I'm here to help. What brought you here to check out our product?"

The executive replies with the problem she's trying to solve.

HereToHelpBot: "Got it. We can help you with that! There are hundreds of companies using our product for that same reason. Would you like to set up a demo (with a human) so you can learn more?"

When the executive replies, "Yes," a calendar appears in the conversation window, with all of the available time slots highlighted, and she's able to schedule a demo for the very next day.

HereToHelpBot: "OK, last step: What email address should I send the calendar invite to?"

And just like that, you've automated the lead capture and qualification processes with a chatbot. When your marketers and sales reps get into the office Monday morning, that demo the executive booked will be there on a sales rep's calendar. For that sales rep, it feels like magic—a demo with a qualified lead just appearing on his calendar overnight. And to think your company used to let those types of leads slip away.

Chatbots: They've Got Our Backs

Ideally, you could always have real people talking to potential customers on your website via messaging. But for most companies, providing 24-hour messaging coverage just isn't feasible. And while chatbot-to-human interactions are no replacement for human-to-human interactions, having chatbots fill in the gaps in your messaging schedule is certainly better than ignoring your leads during those hours when your team is offline.

Today, chatbots have become the concierges of company websites. In a world where so many business-to-business (B2B) and software-as-a-service (SaaS) companies are treating their websites like empty stores, the rise of chatbots means we can now greet our website visitors and engage with them in real time at any hour, day or night. Today's chatbots can route visitors to the right departments, ask qualifying questions (see Figure 3.1), help qualified leads book meetings with sales reps, and—

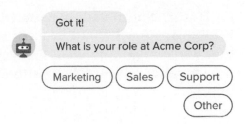

FIGURE 3.1 Chatbots can ask visitors the same qualifying questions your sales team would ask.

after integrating with your company's knowledge base or help desk—can even answer basic questions about your product.

While some people have considered (and perhaps still consider) chatbots to be annoying or ineffective or otherwise unsuitable as a channel for business communication, attitudes have been shifting. A 2016 report by Pingup found that nearly 50% of people who've engaged with a company's chatbot reported having a positive experience. And when they looked at millennials in particular, they found that 55% reported having a positive experience after engaging with a company's chatbot.

Before we dive deeper into how your marketing and sales team can use chatbots to deliver a real-time, on-demand buying experience at scale, let's take a quick look back at how chatbot technology has evolved over the years and explore why businesses can no longer afford to ignore it.

A Brief History of Chatbots

A chatbot is a computer program that's been designed to communicate the way humans prefer to communicate: through conversations. For decades, computer scientists have been working on the problem of natural language processing (NLP), which is a technical way of saying they've been trying to teach computer programs to understand and manipulate human language. That's how chatbots got their start. Specifically, we can trace the origins of chatbots back to 1950, which was the year famed computer scientist, mathematician, and code breaker Alan Turing proposed a now-legendary experiment: the Turing test.

The Turing Test

In his groundbreaking 1950 paper, "Computing Machinery and Intelligence," Turing theorized that a truly intelligent machine would be indistinguishable from a human during a text-only conservation. So in order to put a machine's intelligence to the test, you would need to set up an experiment whereby a participant exchanges messages, in real time, with an unseen party. In some cases that unseen party is another human, and in other cases it's a computer program. If the participant is unable to distinguish the computer program from the human, that computer program is said to have passed the Turing test and can be considered intelligent.

In modern iterations of the experiment, developers compete against one another to see who can build the most convincingly human chatbot, and passing the Turing test requires having your chatbot fool 30% of judges. (Fun fact: During a Turing test competition in 2014, a chatbot named Eugene Goostman was able to convince 33% of the competition's judges that it was actually a 13-year-old Ukrainian boy.)

Turing's ideas laid the groundwork for figuring out how chatbots could function, and for determining the threshold for when a chatbot could be considered intelligent. But back when Turing proposed his test, there were no chatbots or computer programs around that could actually take it. By 1966, however, things had changed.

The First Generation of Chatbots

Developed at the Massachusetts Institute of Technology (M.I.T.) between 1964 and 1966, ELIZA was the world's first chatbot. Programmed by computer scientist Joseph Weizenbaum to simulate the responses of a psychotherapist, ELIZA could carry on convincingly human conversations, at least for short bursts. These conversations could be so convincing, in fact, that Weizenbaum's secretary would ask to spend time alone with the chatbot—not as part of an experiment, but just because she enjoyed talking to it.

In 1973, ELIZA participated in the first-ever conversation between two chatbots. The other chatbot, PARRY, was developed by psychiatrist Kenneth Colby at Stanford University. Fittingly (given ELIZA's programming to respond like a psychotherapist), PARRY was programmed to simulate a person with paranoid schizophrenia.

While the chatbots that comprised this first generation were never able to pass the Turing test, they proved that chatbots could still successfully engage people in conversation, even if their responses didn't always make perfect sense.

Chatbots in the Age of Artificial Intelligence (AI)

In the 1980s, computer scientists began using a new type of AI technology, known as machine learning, to power chatbots. With machine learning, chatbots gained the ability to learn from experience—just as a person can. The more conversations these chatbots have, the better they become at communicating and sounding human.

One of the first-ever machine learning-powered chatbots was Jabberwacky, which was created by programmer Rollo Carpenter in 1988. Originally designed to "simulate natural human chat in an interesting, entertaining and humorous manner," different iterations of Jabberwacky would go on to win Carpenter the Loebner Prize (a Turing test competition) in 2005 and again in 2006.

With the rise of machine learning came a new wave of intelligent chatbots. These chatbots were capable of not only carrying on conversations but also learning from those conversations and constantly improving.

Chatbots in the Internet Age

As access to the internet became increasingly widespread, with it came broader access to chatbots. One of the first online chatbots that people were able to engage with was called A.L.I.C.E. (full name: Artificial Linguistic Internet Computer Entity), which programmer Richard Wallace debuted in 1995. An online version of Jabberwacky, meanwhile, became available in 1997. Unlike Jabberwacky, however, A.L.I.C.E. did not use machine learning. Instead, it relied solely on pattern matching against a static database. In other words, it could talk, but it couldn't learn to talk better—at least not without being reprogrammed. Still, the chatbot was able to win the Loebner Prize in 2000, 2001, and 2004.

The biggest takeaway from this era of chatbots: The internet made it possible for one-to-one, human-to-chatbot conversations to happen at scale. This was the era when people all around the world were able to become more familiar with chatbots. One of those people was filmmaker Spike Jonze, whose conversations with A.L.I.C.E. helped inspire his 2013 film *Her*, which is about a human who has lengthy conversations with—and ultimately falls in love with—a computer program.

Chatbots in the Age of Messaging

While the rise of the internet allowed chatbots to become more widely available to the general public, the rise of messaging allowed chatbots to become useful.

In 2001, back during the first wave of messaging, a chatbot by the name of SmarterChild joined the buddy lists of millions of AOL Instant Messenger (AIM) and MSN Messenger users. Like its predecessors, SmarterChild could successfully engage people in conversation. But in addition to being a source of entertainment, SmarterChild could, on request, provide information about news, sports, or the weather, and it had built-in tools and games that users could access instantly. SmarterChild was sort of like a text-based version of Apple's Siri—only the former debuted about ten years before the latter.

At its peak, SmarterChild was receiving hundreds of millions of messages per day, and conversations with

SmarterChild accounted for 5% of all instant messaging traffic (according to a 2016 VentureBeat article by Robert Hoffer, one of SmarterChild's creators). Thanks in part to the rise of messaging—and in part to the fact that it was actually useful—SmarterChild, during its time, was able to become the most popular chatbot in history.

Today, thousands of chatbot developers are now following SmarterChild's pioneering playbook. They're building chatbots that provide real value, and they're building them on top of messaging. As Hoffer wrote in 2016, "Instant Messaging was and remains an excellent platform for launching applications. . . . IM rocks as an application platform because the most common way we communicate is in fact text."

Facebook, which opened up Facebook Messenger to chatbot developers in 2016, appears to agree with Hoffer's assessment. Within three months of launching their Messenger Platform, developers had already built 11,000 chatbots on top of Messenger, which included chatbots that could order flowers (1–800-Flowers), schedule rides (Uber), and check the weather (Poncho). At the time, Facebook was actually playing catch-up, as rival messaging services like Telegram, Kik, and Line had already launched chatbot platforms of their own.

In addition to being available on messaging platforms where we talk to friends and family, chatbots are now available on messaging-based collaboration tools like Slack. There are hundreds of chatbots you can use inside of Slack for anything from getting updates about your latest marketing and sales metrics to booking business travel to taking team-wide polls and surveys.

Thanks to the rise of messaging, which provided the perfect platform for chatbots to flourish, chatbots are now more than just intellectual curiosities: They're valuable tools that individuals—and businesses—can use to drive real outcomes.

According to the 2016 study by Pingup I cited earlier, nearly 30% of people who've used chatbots on messaging platforms have used them to communicate with businesses.

Chatbots and Humans: Finding the Perfect Balance

Regardless of how you personally feel about chatbots, there are two facts that can't be ignored: (1) People are using chatbots and (2) Chatbots *can* be useful . . . provided you use them correctly.

At Drift, our philosophy when it comes to using chatbots for marketing and sales is to get them out of people's way as soon as possible. The chatbots we put on our website aren't there to entertain people or to waste their time, they're there to help people and to save them time. What's more, we never try to pass our chatbots off as human. While the Turing test has conditioned generations of developers into thinking that the goal of building a chatbot should be to have it perfectly simulate a human during conversation, I don't really think of it like that. At Drift, our goal is to build chatbots that can solve specific problems (and solving those problems usually doesn't require that chatbots be able to trick people into thinking they're human).

A Modern Approach to Understanding AI

Traditional definitions of AI are rooted in this notion that human intelligence should be the measuring stick. So if we want to determine whether a machine is intelligent, we test to see whether it can do things that humans need intelligence to do.

A separate camp of AI researchers, however, argue that framing AI as a quest to understand and imitate human intelligence is the wrong approach. They argue that the goal of AI shouldn't be to build computer programs and chatbots that can behave like humans but to build computer programs and chatbots that can solve problems creatively, and that can maximize their chances of success toward achieving some goal.

That's exactly how we think about the chatbots we build at Drift, where we use the power of machine learning not to make our chatbots more human-like, but to make them better at the tasks they're performing. And that's why the notion that chatbots could someday replace marketers and salespeople is misplaced: We're not building chatbots that can do everything humans can do, we're building chatbots that can automate those tedious and repetitive tasks that humans hate doing.

Chatbots *and* Humans (Not Chatbots *Versus* Humans)

Using chatbots as part of your marketing and sales strategy isn't about replacing humans, it's about supplementing your human workforce and helping them do their jobs as efficiently as possible. And in a world where billions of people now prefer to communicate via messaging and have come to expect a real-time buying experience by default, most marketing and sales teams could use that extra help that chatbots can provide.

In addition to being the perfect solution for keeping messaging—your website's real-time lead generation channel—up and running on nights and weekends, chatbots can help you manage conversations during the day. This becomes especially helpful during times when you have an influx of visitors to your website and are struggling to respond to everyone. In cases like those, a chatbot can automatically jump in and let people know that you'll be with them shortly. Granted, in a subset of those cases, the chatbot will be able to resolve a person's problem in a few seconds, before you ever have the chance to chat (see Figure 3.2).

While I personally want my marketing and sales teams to have human-to-human conversations with as many customers and potential customers as possible, I also understand that sometimes people are just looking for quick answers. So instead of forcing them to stick around and talk, we can cater the experience to their needs by using chatbots to provide self-service access to the information they're looking for.

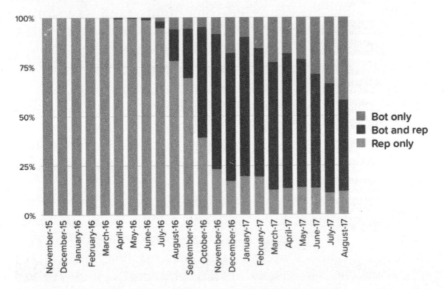

Hey! I'm loving the product so far. I've got a question about what I can customize.

Bot

Hey there! While we wait for someone to jump in, we found some links that may be helpful:

1. Customizing your colors
2. Customizing your button
3. How to Customize in Settings

FIGURE 3.2 Chatbots can provide speedy responses to common product questions.

Since incorporating chatbots into our marketing and sales strategy, the way we engage with website visitors at Drift has evolved dramatically (see Figure 3.3). Of the 20% of people who start conversations with us via messaging, 48% of those conversations are now being managed solely by chatbots.

FIGURE 3.3 A breakdown of how conversations are managed on the Drift website.

We've gone from having humans manage 100% of our incoming conversations on their own to now having them manage just 10% of conversations on their own. The remaining chunk of conversations (around 40%) are managed by a combination of chatbots and humans.

It's a team effort, just as marketing and sales has always been a team effort. By adding a chatbot to that team, you'll be able to deliver a real-time, on-demand buying experience at scale.

How Chatbots Enable a Better Buying Experience

In a 2018 report that Drift published in partnership with SurveyMonkey Audience, Salesforce, and myclever, we uncovered the most common frustrations that consumers face when it comes to traditional online experiences (see Figure 3.4). At the top of the list: websites being hard

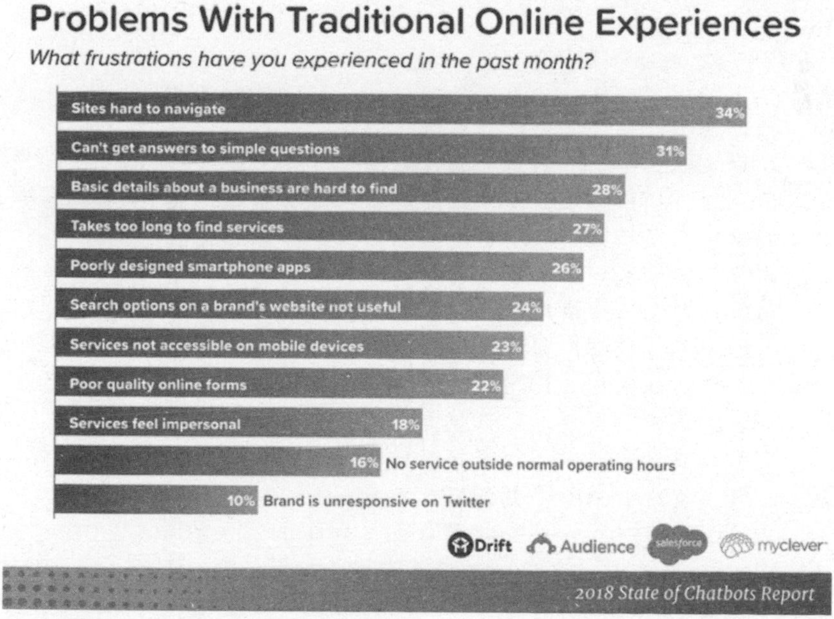

Problems With Traditional Online Experiences

What frustrations have you experienced in the past month?

Sites hard to navigate	34%
Can't get answers to simple questions	31%
Basic details about a business are hard to find	28%
Takes too long to find services	27%
Poorly designed smartphone apps	26%
Search options on a brand's website not useful	24%
Services not accessible on mobile devices	23%
Poor quality online forms	22%
Services feel impersonal	18%
No service outside normal operating hours	16%
Brand is unresponsive on Twitter	10%

Drift Audience salesforce myclever

2018 State of Chatbots Report

FIGURE 3.4 Businesses are making it hard for buyers to find the information they're looking for.

to navigate (34%). This was followed by not being able to get answers to simple questions (31%), and basic details about a business, like address, hours of operations, and phone number, being difficult to find (28%).

When you look at these top three frustrations—poor website navigation, not being able to get answers to simple questions, and basic company details being hard to find—you can see that they all point to the same underlying problem: Buyers are struggling, and failing, to gain access to the information they need from your website.

By adding a chatbot to your website that could serve as a personal concierge for buyers, you'd no longer have to worry about buyers becoming tangled up in your website's navigation. Buyers could start conversations with the chatbot and get access to a centralized source of information from any page on your website. And provided you sync your chatbot with your company's knowledge base or help desk, buyers would always be able to find answers to basic questions about your product. Best of all, because this would all happen over messaging, buyers would be able to get those answers in real time, 24 hours a day, seven days a week.

Millennial Buyers Versus Baby Boomer Buyers

As part of that same 2018 report I mentioned above, we asked consumers what they considered to be the biggest benefits of chatbots when it came to their potential for improving traditional online experiences. Overall, 64% said receiving 24-hour service, making it the top expected benefit of chatbots. In second and third place came getting instant responses and getting answers to simple questions, both with 55%.

When we looked at that same data, but this time organized by age groups, we were surprised to learn that it wasn't just millennials who had such high expectations for chatbots: baby boomers saw the benefits as well (see Figure 3.5). In fact, while more millennials saw 24-hour service as a potential benefit of chatbots (66% versus 58%), more baby boomers agreed that getting answers to simple

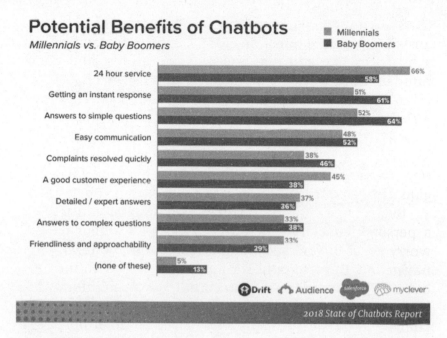

Potential Benefits of Chatbots
Millennials vs. Baby Boomers

■ Millennials
■ Baby Boomers

	Millennials	Baby Boomers
24 hour service	66%	58%
Getting an instant response	51%	61%
Answers to simple questions	52%	64%
Easy communication	48%	52%
Complaints resolved quickly	38%	46%
A good customer experience	45%	38%
Detailed / expert answers	37%	26%
Answers to complex questions	33%	38%
Friendliness and approachability	33%	29%
(none of these)	5%	13%

Drift   Audience   salesforce   myclever

2018 State of Chatbots Report

FIGURE 3.5 Millennials and baby boomers alike are seeing the potential benefits of chatbots.

questions was a potential benefit (64% versus 52%) *and* that getting instant responses was a potential benefit (61% versus 51%). The takeaway here: chatbots aren't just for millennials. They have the potential to improve online experiences for all buyers, regardless of their age.

Potential Blockers to Chatbot Adoption

Of course, not all buyers are ready to abandon human-to-human interactions entirely, and some aren't sure they trust chatbots to perform certain tasks. In our 2018 study, we found that 43% of consumers would prefer to talk to a human over a chatbot and that 30% would worry about chatbots making a mistake (such as during a purchase or while making a reservation). Meanwhile, 27% of consumers agreed that only being able to use chatbots on a single platform, such as Facebook, would be a deterrent to adoption (see Figure 3.6).

Potential Blockers to Using Chatbots
What would stop you from using a chatbot?

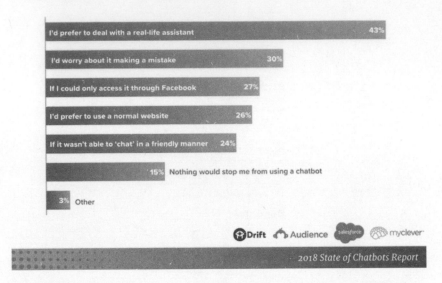

I'd prefer to deal with a real-life assistant	43%
I'd worry about it making a mistake	30%
If I could only access it through Facebook	27%
I'd prefer to use a normal website	26%
If it wasn't able to 'chat' in a friendly manner	24%
15% Nothing would stop me from using a chatbot	
3% Other	

Drift · Audience · salesforce · myclever

2018 State of Chatbots Report

FIGURE 3.6 43% of buyers would prefer to talk to a person instead of a chatbot.

The good news: As a business, it doesn't have to be either/or. You can have chatbots handle the tasks that chatbots are good at handling, such as answering basic questions in real time, 24 hours a day, while the humans on your team can handle the tasks that humans are good at handling, like providing in-depth explanations of how your product works. What's more, you don't have to force your buyers to sign up for a specific messaging service in order for them to be able to interact with a chatbot. By adding messaging to your website, and then adding chatbots on top of that messaging platform, any website visitor will be able to receive the concierge-level service that chatbots can now provide.

How a Single Marketer Can Book Meetings for Dozens of Sales Reps Using Chatbots

So far, we've primarily explored how chatbots can be used for *reactive* tasks in order to improve a buyer's experience, such as greeting people when they land on your website, providing immediate responses to simple questions, and allowing inbound leads to effectively qualify themselves and book meetings. Ultimately, one of the overarching benefits of adding chatbots to your website is that they scale the ability to be helpful to the people who are already dropping by.

As management consultant Brad Power wrote in the *Harvard Business Review* in 2017: "When it comes to AI in business, a machine doesn't have to fool people; it doesn't have to pass the Turing test; it just needs to help them and thereby help the businesses that deploy them. And that test has already been passed."

Power went on to write that during an interview with a company's chief marketing officer (CMO), the CMO told him, "AI tools are the only way I can scale 'helpfulness' to a global community of 200,000-plus users with a team of two.'"

For small marketing teams, the simple addition of messaging and chatbots to your website can produce immediate results, as you'll be able to catch leads that had been slipping through the cracks. Unlike humans, which can only engage with a handful of website visitors simultaneously, chatbots can engage with hundreds, thousands, or potentially even millions of visitors simultaneously, which means the experience is easily scalable.

Using Chatbots Proactively

Of course, chatbots aren't useful only when serving as intelligent safety nets for your website. Marketing teams can also use them to seek out new opportunities for Sales.

By creating custom hyperlinks that trigger chatbot conversations, and then sharing those links on social media, or in emails, or wherever you want to share them, you can proactively start adding new leads to your sales funnel. Depending on how you configure your chatbot, the next step could be to have those leads answer a few qualifying questions, and then the qualified leads could be given the opportunity to schedule meetings on a sales rep's calendar.

This entire process, from the time a lead clicks your link to the time that lead books a meeting with a sales rep, can take just a few seconds, and it requires zero intervention on the part of your sales reps. In fact, there are really only two things salespeople are on the hook for here. First, they need to connect their calendars so the chatbot can let qualified leads schedule meetings with them. And second, they need to show up for those meetings. Apart from that, a single marketer can set up the chatbot (without having to write any code) and manage the entire process.

Keeping reading to learn the ins and outs of how you can do the same for your business.

Chapter 4

Replacing Lead Capture Forms with Conversations

By adding messaging to their websites, marketers and salespeople gained the ability to capture and qualify leads through having real-time conversations. By adding chatbots, they gained the ability to scale that experience and to keep their websites open for business 24 hours a day.

Finally, marketers and salespeople have the tools they need in order to prevent their websites from becoming "empty stores." Business-to-business (B2B) companies can finally catch up to the business-to-consumer (B2C) world and start providing the real-time, on-demand buying experience today's customers have come to expect. Just imagine a world where going through the B2B buying process feels like buying a book from Amazon, or streaming a video on Netflix, or scheduling a ride with Uber or Lyft. That's where we're headed, and messaging and chatbots can help us get there.

Lead capture forms, on the other hand, have been holding us back. They are relics from an earlier marketing and sales paradigm, back before owning the demand became more important than owning the supply, and before the balance of power shifted from company to customer. Today, any company can install messaging and chatbots on their website in just a few minutes by simply copying and pasting a snippet of code. So why are so many of us still relying on lead capture forms? Why are we still putting up roadblocks and making potential customers wait when we could be having conversations with them instead?

Adapting to changes in the way your customers prefer to buy isn't only about taking advantage of the latest advancements in technology, it's also about knowing when to stop using outdated technology.

The Problems with Lead Capture Forms

Lead capture forms have an average of 11 form fields, according to a 2015 report by Formstack. That's 11 questions companies are forcing people to answer before they can... what? Download some slides you designed in PowerPoint? Get a callback from a sales rep? The notion that we would demand that people give us information about themselves before we'll agree to talk to them or share information with them is completely antithetical to taking a customer-driven approach to business. In a world where customers have all the power, where information has become increasingly democratized, and where people have come to expect companies to be as helpful as possible, lead capture forms stick out like a sore thumb: they make it harder for people to access the information they're looking for.

That brings us to the first of four main problems I see with lead capture forms:

Problem 1. Forms Are Roadblocks, Stopping Buyers in Their Tracks

Consider this hypothetical: A potential customer hears about your product from a friend. She does some research, reads some reviews, and then heads to your website. She reads a few blog posts and is intrigued by a "free" guide you're promoting that offers tips and best practices for using your product. But when she tries to read it, BAM: She runs into a lead capture form.

Now, imagine this same potential customer decides that she's read enough of your content and is ready to schedule a demo with Sales so she can see your product in action. But when she clicks the "Contact Sales" or "Schedule Demo" button on your website, she's directed to a landing page where BAM: She runs into another lead capture form.

As marketers and salespeople, we should be making the buying process as seamless as possible for the people visiting our websites. By using forms, we're doing the opposite. Instead of engaging potential customers in real time, while they're on our websites and at their most interested, we're stopping them in their tracks and then forcing them into annoying email back-and-forths and never-ending games of phone tag. This leads us to problem number two.

Problem 2. The Follow-Up Experience Is Terrible

Many of today's savviest tech buyers have set up separate email addresses that they use specifically for content downloads and form-fills. Why? Because they want to shield themselves from what comes *after* they fill out those lead capture forms: emails, emails, and more emails.

As marketers and salespeople, the traditional approach to capturing and qualifying leads on our websites (see Figure 4.1) starts with getting people to fill out forms.

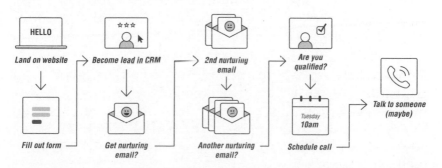

FIGURE 4.1 An outdated playbook for capturing and qualifying leads.

Everything hinges on that initial form-fill. Then the leads we capture with forms get added to our customer relationship management (CRM) or automation systems and we can begin "nurturing" them with emails.

Instead of letting our potential customers decide how they interact with us, the traditional playbook has us deciding for them. And instead of responding to leads in real-time, the traditional playbook has us wait and follow up later. That's assuming, of course, that we bother to follow up at all.

As the former VP of demand generation at Workable, John Short, told the Drift marketing team, today's tech buyers are losing faith in forms. In particular, when it comes to filling out a form in order to get in touch with a sales rep, buyers can no longer be certain they'll get a response. And that's one of the main reasons why John decided to replace Workable's forms with real-time conversations. As he told us, "We wanted to increase the number of people reaching out to request demos and pricing. We hypothesized that people don't fill out forms because they don't think they will get contacted." (Our research at Drift backs this up. As I mentioned in Chapter One, our lead response survey found that 58% of B2B companies don't respond to sales inquiries.)

By using a combination of messaging and chatbots, Workable has been able to eliminate the terrible follow-up experiences that come with using lead forms and can now respond to all of their leads in real time. As John explained, "It's critical for our users that we respond within seconds. Average time on page for us is about three minutes, so if someone starts a conversation and they have to wait two minutes, then that's a long time for them."

Of course, speedy response times aren't just good from a customer experience perspective: They're good for your business's bottom line as well. As John told us, after replacing forms with conversations, "The benefit is that you'll see conversion rates increase both from visit-to-lead and from lead-to-customer."

Problem 3. Forms Don't Work As Well As They Used To

Back in the early days of online marketing and sales, lead capture forms made a lot of sense. They provided companies with an easy-to-use mechanism for collecting contact information at scale. Using the old "form and follow-up" approach, one or two marketers could capture thousands of leads, score and segment those leads, and then bombard them with emails.

For years, marketing and sales teams have depended on forms in order to make the lead qualification process scalable. But these days, forms just aren't that effective anymore. As I shared in Chapter One, 81% of today's tech buyers don't bother filling out forms when they encounter gated content. Meanwhile, the average landing page form conversion rate has dropped to just 2.35%.

Back when SalesRabbit was using lead capture forms and email exchanges (between lead and sales rep) in order to schedule sales demos, the company was seeing 25% of their demo requests convert into actual demos delivered. When they replaced forms with real-time conversations (powered by messaging and chatbots), that conversion rate quickly grew by 40%. What's more, the number of qualified leads they were generating grew by nearly 50%. When using forms, SalesRabbit saw approximately 15% of their leads eventually move to a lead status of "not interested." After replacing forms with conversations, that figure dropped to 8%.

By giving potential customers the option of being able to schedule demos in real time, SalesRabbit opened up a fast lane for their best leads. They no longer had to put roadblocks in the buying process with forms or subject leads to the terrible experience that typically followed form-fills. As Ben Nettesheim, senior director of Digital Marketing at SalesRabbit, told the Drift marketing team: "It was a welcomed change. The sales team was now spending more of their valuable time working demos and less time playing phone or email tag to schedule those demos."

Problem 4. Forms Are Static and Impersonal

One final argument for why lead capture forms have become outdated: They don't treat potential customers like people, they treat them like contacts in a database. While this might seem like a frivolous point, it's important to remember that every interaction a person has with your company and your brand shapes his or her overall experience. And when one of the very first interactions a person has is being forced to hand over contact information in exchange for content, or a phone call, it doesn't make for a great start.

Unlike a chatbot, or a person using messaging, a lead capture form can't answer questions. It can't route you to the right department. It can't help you find a time on a sales rep's calendar. And while it can "ask" questions with its 11 form fields, it can't ask them conversationally, which leads to the overall experience feeling cold and impersonal. For companies that are trying to create an enjoyable buying experience, this can be a major problem. As Rich Wood, managing director of Six & Flow, told the Drift marketing team: "Personality and humor is a big part of who we are and how we work in the Six & Flow office. It's incredibly difficult to show either in a form . . . forms basically suck the fun from the page."

With messaging and chatbots, however, marketing and sales teams can let their personalities shine through, and they can treat people like actual people (and not like contacts in a database). By replacing forms with conversations, companies can deliver a more human buying experience and, in the process, get closer to their customers.

How the #NoForms Movement Got Its Start

In April of 2016, I called Drift's head of marketing, Dave Gerhardt, and gave him the news. Right away, because I had called him instead of using Slack, he knew it was going to be something important. That being said, he definitely wasn't prepared to hear what I had to say. Our conversation went something like this:

Me: "Hey, you got a second?"

DG: "Sure, what's up?"

Me: "I think we should get rid of all our forms and make our content free.

(Silence.)

DG: "Uh . . . OK."

Needless to say, he wasn't immediately convinced. As a marketer, he had been trained to use lead capture forms to supply Sales with as many leads as possible. For years, that *was* marketing. The goal was to drive people to your website so you could get them to trade information about themselves for content (like ebooks, white papers, or email courses), which you would keep locked up behind lead capture forms.

However, as I explained to Dave, when you take a step back and look at what we've been doing, and how we've been treating our potential customers, it's clear that marketing has lost its way. We've forgotten how important it is to truly connect with people and to tell an authentic story. Instead, we've become obsessed with churning out as much content as possible and doing search engine optimization (SEO) in order to have that content rank for this keyword and that keyword. Instead of focusing on the experience people are having when they interact with us, we've been focusing on gaming the system. We've been treating marketing like a get-rich-quick scheme.

Lead capture forms are a byproduct of this old way of thinking. They make it easy for marketers and salespeople to collect contact information at scale, but the resulting experience for the buyer is terrible. So without giving it too much more thought than that, we pulled the plug. We took down our lead capture forms and made all of our content free. Next, we worked to figure out how we could capture and qualify leads on our website without using forms—and that's really when conversational marketing and sales, as a methodology, began to take shape. It wasn't part of some preconceived master plan: We were simply following a customer-driven approach to running our business, and conversational marketing and sales is where that approach led us.

The Movement Gains Momentum

As we experimented with using messaging and chatbots to capture and qualify leads in real time, without forms, we shared our progress using the hashtag #NoForms and encouraged others to do the same. We also took a page out of Salesforce's playbook, which once designed a "No Software" logo—the word "Software" in a red circle with a line through it—to promote how different their product was from traditional software products. In our version, we've set the word "Forms" in the red circle with the line through it (see Figure 4.2), and we printed out thousands of stickers to share with marketers and salespeople who joined us in our mission to replace forms with conversations.

One of the earliest people to join us in the #NoForms movement was Tom Wentworth, chief marketing officer (CMO) at the data science software company Rapid-Miner. RapidMiner has tens of thousands of people dropping by their website every month. Some of them are first-time visitors, some of them are free users, and some of them are paying customers. But what they all have in common, as RapidMiner CMO Tom Wentworth told the Drift marketing team in an interview, is that they're coming to the RapidMiner website for a reason:

FIGURE 4.2 Drift's "No Forms" logo (inspired by Salesforce's "No Software" logo).

"People who come to our website aren't coming there because they want to surf our site, they're coming there because they have a specific problem, whether it's a question about our product or what it does, whether it's some technical support they need, or whether it's they want to talk to someone in sales."

Using the traditional approach to marketing and sales, of course, Tom could have simply made all of those people coming to the RapidMiner website fill out lead forms and wait for follow-ups. But when he thought about the overall experience RapidMiner was trying to provide, he realized that the traditional approach just wasn't cutting it anymore.

As he explained: "If we build great products our objective should be to get users to use our great products and to then support them in that journey. And that is not a marketing journey that starts with a form on a website that leads to a content download that leads to a barrage of emails. As a marketer, my job isn't as much about marketing as it is about teaching and enabling."

How RapidMiner Replaced Forms with Real-Time Conversations

Instead of relying on forms and follow-ups, Tom decided that RapidMiner should engage with their website visitors in real time, while they were live on the website and at their most interested. So he added messaging to the RapidMiner website and tagged in the sales team to manage the incoming conversations. However, because there were tens of thousands of visitors coming to the RapidMiner website each month, sorting through all of the conversations and trying to identify leads soon proved impossible. The volume of incoming conversations was simply too high for the sales team to handle. They were overwhelmed.

That's when Tom added a chatbot to his website (see Figure 4.3), and it was as if he had found the missing piece of the puzzle. In addition to acting as a personal concierge for website visitors, the chatbot serves as an intelligent

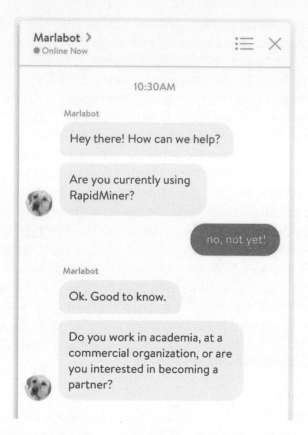

FIGURE 4.3 A screenshot of RapidMiner's lead qualification chatbot, Marlabot, in action.

switchboard for the sales team, ensuring only the best leads get through.

As Tom explained: "If the bot uncovers that someone's ready for a sales conversation, we can connect them to our sales team. If the bot uncovers that someone has a question about a particular product feature, we can bring in one of our product specialists. So the bot really helps to narrow that conversation and we can then bring it forward to the right person."

To clarify, Tom didn't start using chatbots in order to remove humans from RapidMiner's marketing and sales process. Instead, he started using them in order to make it easier for visitors, leads, and customers to get in touch with the right people at the right time. And through automating the lead qualification process, he's able to free up his team so they can focus on providing a great experience. As Tom explained, "Our marketing team now spends most of our time finding new ways to help our users, rather than how to annoy them with more email nurture campaigns and lead collection forms."

Within the first few months of having messaging and chatbots live on the RapidMiner website, Tom was able to capture more than 4,000 leads through this new, real-time channel. Conversations soon became the source of 10% of RapidMiner's new sales pipeline and influenced 25% of open sales pipeline (worth more than $1 million). All of this growth, and no lead capture forms in sight.

Rethinking Our Content and Lead Generation Strategies

For those who have been disciplined students of inbound marketing and content marketing for the past several years, the idea of ungating content and replacing lead capture forms with conversations might sound a bit out there. After all, marketing teams are typically evaluated based on how many leads they're able to generate, and they typically generate those leads using gated content. Here's how it works: First, marketing teams publish free, short-form content, like blog posts, driving as much traffic to those posts as possible. Then, they add calls-to-action (CTAs) to those blog posts that drive people to landing pages that house longer-form, gated content, like ebooks.

Under this old system, marketing teams would effectively game the system by generating as much high-ranking, short-form content as possible so they could drive as many visitors as possible to their landing pages. Specifically, marketing teams began covering a broader and broader array of topics, some of which had little or no connection to the service their company was providing, and became obsessed with writing click-bait headlines. Instead of serving as trustworthy resources that potential customers could turn to, many marketing teams turned into content farms.

Why Content Is More Powerful Without Forms

When you ungate your content, the goals of your content strategy suddenly shift. Instead of having to obsess over creating content that will generate leads, you can obsess over creating content that will resonate with potential customers and add real value. And instead of treating long-form content as something you can use as leverage for obtaining someone's email address, you can think of it as something you can use to build your brand and to tell an authentic story.

For example, one of the first things we did at Drift after getting rid of forms was to self-publish a book (*Hypergrowth*), which we made available—for free—in several different formats. In less than a month, more than 3,000 people had downloaded it and another 4,000 had read the version embedded on our landing page. From the very beginning, we treated the book as an opportunity to spread the Drift brand and to provide actionable advice for helping companies become more customer-driven. Instead of focusing on the sheer number of leads we could capture, we focused on creating a great experience and on making the information we were sharing as easy as possible for people to access.

Developing a Form-Free Content Strategy

After launching the book, the feedback we received from our customers and potential customers was incredible. And guess what? Even without using forms, we were *still* able to generate leads, because when people came to our website to read the book, some of them would inevitably start conversations with us via our messaging widget. We could also proactively greet people who were on the book's landing page with personalized messages, which thanked them for checking out the book and let them know we were available to answer any questions they might have.

Meanwhile, back on our blog, we stuck to a schedule of publishing just one to two high-quality posts per week. In a world where some B2B companies are publishing as many as four or five blog posts *per day*, this was a major departure from the norm. But because we had removed our forms and no longer needed to treat content as a lead generation channel, we could focus on the quality of our content instead of the quantity, and we could focus on how each and every piece of content we published would contribute to a person's overall experience with our brand. For people who want to stay up-to-date with our latest content, we built a chatbot that can pop up on our blog and subscribe them to our email newsletter. So while at one point it might have seemed impossible for marketers to be able to drive value from content without having lead forms be part of the equation, today that's no longer the case.

Replacing Marketing-Qualified Leads (MQLs) with Conversation-Qualified Leads (CQLs)

For companies that power their marketing and sales strategies with lead capture forms, one of the most common metrics they track is marketing-qualified leads (MQLs). An MQL is someone who matches your marketing team's target criteria, which is usually based on some combination of demographics, firmographics, and behavior (like downloading an ebook). In other words, MQLs are people who have filled out lead capture forms and who, at least on paper, look a lot like your company's buyer persona—a composite of your ideal buyer.

A common offshoot of the MQL is the sales-qualified lead (SQL). SQLs are essentially MQLs but with a few more boxes ticked off. In addition to matching your team's target criteria, SQLs have typically expressed that they are ready to buy soon. So when it comes time to make outbound sales calls, SQLs are the leads that sales reps will call first.

For companies that offer a free or freemium version of their product, like we do at Drift, product-qualified leads (PQLs) are another metric we've typically tracked. And while many PQLs—free users who are spending time inside your product—do end up converting into paying customers, product usage alone doesn't guarantee that someone's a good fit to buy. Without knowing the *intent* of a lead, without understanding a lead's underlying reasons for wanting to buy, it seems hard to consider that lead qualified.

Introducing the Conversation-Qualified Lead (CQL)

The reason why MQLs, SQLs, and PQLs all ultimately fail as metrics and as systems for measuring lead quality is that they're all based on external observation. They rely on looking at people's behaviors, from a distance, and drawing conclusions from the data you're able to collect.

At Drift, after we replaced our lead capture forms with conversations, we quickly discovered that there was a better way to figure out whether a lead was ready to buy: We'd ask. Instead of forcing people to fill out forms, we'd engage with them right away, in real time. And after we understood why they were there, what problems they were trying to solve, and how they were planning on using our product to solve those problems, we could make an informed conclusion about whether or not they'd be a good fit. The ones who were a good fit we called conversation-qualified leads, or CQLs (see Table 4.1).

A CQL is someone who has expressed intent to buy during a one-to-one conversation with either (a) an employee at your company or (b) an intelligent chatbot. Unlike MQLs, SQLs, and PQLs, CQLs are based on what your potential customers are actually telling you, not on your assumptions. And because those conversations happen in real time, CQLs end up moving through your marketing and sales funnel at lightning speed.

TABLE 4.1	The different categories of qualified leads.
Marketing-Qualified Leads (MQLs)	They look like they could be interested in buying.
Sales-Qualified Leads (SQLs)	Sales has confirmed it: They're interested in buying.
Product-Qualified Leads (PQLs)	They tried our product? They must be interested in buying!
Conversation-Qualified Leads (CQLs)	We talked to them: They told us why they're interested in buying and what they're trying to accomplish with our product.

As Chris Willis, former CMO at Perfecto Mobile, told the Drift marketing team, "Leads that come in through chat tend to have a higher velocity. So you're able to solve the problem or meet the needs of the request in real time. So you think in terms of somebody coming to a website, and having a question, and filling in a contact us form. And they'll hear back in 24 hours, or two days... that problem might not be there anymore. If they're able to initiate a conversation, so skip the form, and have a conversation in real time, we're seeing that move very quickly."

As you'll discover in Chapter Five, giving leads the option to "skip the form" will not only help shorten your sales cycle, but it will also help you strengthen marketing and sales alignment.

Chapter 5

Ending the Family Feud Between Marketing and Sales

Historically, marketing and sales teams haven't had the best track record when it comes to alignment. In many cases, companies have allowed marketing teams and sales teams to operate almost independently of one another. They often have completely separate sets of goals as well as separate philosophies around what the buying experience should look like. Internally, these differences have led to arguments and/or a lack of communication between teams, while externally, they have contributed to a buying experience that can feel bumpy and disjointed.

We saw what this disjointedness looks like first-hand in Chapter Four when we explored how lead capture forms act as roadblocks, forcing buyers to wait and preventing them from reaching out directly to sales reps. From the buyer's perspective, having to fill out a form creates a clear delineation between where the marketing portion of the buying process ends and where the sales portion begins.

While Marketing and Sales are ultimately responsible for the same funnel, and for building relationships with the same people, the way these teams have been operating doesn't always reflect that. Traditionally, Marketing has sat at the top of the funnel, obsessing over generating as many leads as possible for Sales, while Sales has sat at the bottom of the funnel, trying to convert those leads into customers. Have you spotted how this arrangement could cause (and has caused) tension between teams?

A Flawed System: The Ongoing Battle Over Leads

If a sales team fails to hit its target, the traditional arrangement makes it easy for them to point the finger at the marketing team and say, "Hey, those leads you gave us were no good. You didn't set us up for success." The marketing team, meanwhile, can easily counter that accusation by responding, "No, those leads were great; your team just didn't reach out to them fast enough. You did a bad job connecting."

To this day, this battle over leads is happening at companies around the world. In trying to resolve it, we've resorted to things like creating contracts—or service-level agreements (SLAs)—between marketing teams and sales teams, which assert that Marketing will be responsible for generating a certain amount of leads of a certain quality, and that Sales will be responsible for closing a certain amount of those leads. It's a way to hold both teams accountable.

Another solution has been to create a new team that lives in the middle of the funnel, between Marketing and Sales. Depending on the company, the members of this team might be called business development representatives (BDRs), sales development representatives (SDRs), or lead development representatives (LDRs), but the overarching purpose across all of these roles is the same: to identify qualified leads before passing them on to the sales team. You can think of BDRs, SDRs, and LDRs (which I'll refer to simply as BDRs moving forward) as an additional layer in the funnel that helps filter out people who aren't a good fit to buy, thus allowing your sales team to dedicate more of their time to talking to your best leads.

This, however, raises another question: How do you agree on which leads are your best leads? As we learned in the previous chapter, companies typically categorize leads as either being marketing-qualified (MQLs), when leads match the profile of a customer; sales-qualified (SQLs), when leads have shown they're interested in buying soon; and, for companies with free or freemium products, product-qualified (PQLs), when leads have spent time using your product. But as we also saw, all three of these lead types, MQLs, SQLs, and PQLs, fail to take the customer's perspective into account. And they're still tethered to the same, forms-based system that separates Marketing and Sales into two separate experiences for buyers.

How Conversations Bring Marketing and Sales Teams Together

At Drift, after getting rid of our lead capture forms and replacing them with real-time conversations, I soon began to notice an unintended (but positive) side effect: Behind the scenes, the alignment between our marketing and sales teams was getting stronger. Meanwhile, on our website, it was getting harder and harder to figure out where the experience the marketing team was providing ended and where the experience the sales team was providing began.

Instead of focusing on MQLs, SQLs, or PQLs, our marketing and sales teams both became focused on CQLs, or conversation-qualified leads. These were the people on our website we were talking to in real time and gathering information from first-hand, during one-to-one conversations. And because there were no lead capture forms clogging up the buying process, these CQLs were able to move seamlessly through our marketing and sales funnel, sometimes in as little as a few hours. In Figure 5.1, you can see a Slack conversation between Ally (a Drift sales rep), Armen (Drift's head of sales), and Dave (Drift's head of marketing) that showcases just how quickly CQLs can convert into customers—and how Marketing and Sales leaders alike are recognizing the value.

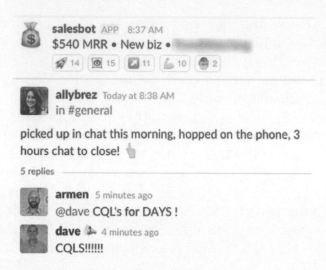

FIGURE 5.1 While leads often take days or weeks to close, conversation-qualified leads (CQLs) can close in hours.

When you remove lead capture forms from the equation, you're not just breaking down a barrier between potential customers and the information (or people) they're trying to gain access to, you're also breaking down a barrier between Marketing and Sales. By removing lead capture forms, you're able to smooth over the bumpiness and disjointedness that comes with the traditional approach, and you're able to blur the line between where Marketing ends and where Sales begins.

Behind the scenes, everyone on both teams can see all of the interactions leads have taken on your website and can review all of the conversations they've had. And thanks to data enrichment, which pulls in relevant information about a lead from LinkedIn and other online sources, a lead's basic details—like what company he or she works at, how many employees that company has, and so on—can be gleaned in an instant. That means skeptical sales reps can now quickly and easily verify that leads are qualified before they dedicate time to talking to them. But more importantly, it means sales reps can always go into conversations with plenty of context.

In the past, the handoff between Marketing and Sales—the passing of leads from the top of the funnel down to the bottom—has been a contentious process. But by reimagining the way we capture and qualify leads on our website, with conversations instead of forms, we've been able to streamline the buying process while simultaneously bringing our marketing and sales functions closer together.

Although to be fair, we didn't do it alone.

Streamlining the Marketing/Sales Handoff with Artificial Intelligence

According to 2016 research from the McKinsey Global Institute, 40% of sales work activities can now be automated using artificial intelligence (AI) and other leading-edge technologies. And as advances in natural language processing (NLP) continue, and intelligent chatbots are able to understand and communicate using human languages more effectively, McKinsey predicts that 47% of sales activities will become automatable. While this might sound ominous to some sales professionals, keep in mind that the sales tasks intelligent chatbots are automating tend to be the same tasks today's sales (and marketing) professionals hate doing, such as manually updating contact records in a customer relationship management (CRM) system. By taking over these types of tasks, chatbots are allowing sales reps to focus more of their time on doing what they do best: building relationships with buyers and closing deals. Chatbots are also freeing up marketers to focus on what they do best: building your company's brand.

The rise of intelligent chatbots has given marketing and sales teams the ability to capture, qualify, and book meetings with leads 24 hours a day, even when sales reps are asleep or away on vacation. Chatbots can also automatically route qualified leads to particular sales reps (or to the calendars of particular sales reps) based on sales territory or whatever routing rules companies want to set. And if there are multiple reps who share ownership of a sales territory, no problem: chatbots can divvy up qualified leads round-robin style, so it's always fair and leads are always distributed evenly.

After integrating with a CRM, such as Salesforce, chatbots can also add the information they gather during conversations directly into contact records, which saves teams from having to waste time on manual data entry. But unlike a lead capture form, a chatbot isn't just some passive data collection tool: It actively engages with people and learns about them through conversation. As RapidMiner's CMO, Tom Wentworth, told the *Harvard Business Review* in regard to his experience using chatbots on the RapidMiner website: "I've learned things about my visitors that no other analytics system would show. We've learned about new use cases, and we've learned about product problems."

In addition to providing sales reps with tons of useful information, chatbots provide qualified leads with the option of moving further along in the buying process by letting them schedule meetings with sales reps. It all happens right there, in a single conversation, and as a result, the "handoff" from Marketing to Sales is rendered nonexistent. For the buyer, it's a completely seamless process.

How Six & Flow Used Chatbots to Enter a New Market

As a UK-based marketing agency that's trying to grow in the B2B technology space, Six & Flow initially struggled to overcome the eight-hour time difference they have with San Francisco, the hub of B2B technology companies. Given the lack of overlap in business hours, Six & Flow sales reps don't have a lot of time each day to talk, human-to-human, to their website visitors (and target customers) from the United States. For years, the solution to this problem, of course, has been to have the marketing team put up lead capture forms so Sales could follow up later. But Six & Flow decided to do something different: They added a chatbot to their website that engages with visitors during the hours they're offline.

After three months of automating their "off hours" with chatbots, Six & Flow saw a 23% increase in leads and a 15% increase in new clients, many of which are based in the U.S. Meanwhile, the length of Six & Flow's sales cycle has dropped by 33%. As the agency's managing director, Rich Wood, explained to the Drift marketing team:

"Having someone out of hours manning the site just isn't cost effective. Our bots help to start conversations, book meetings and show a little bit of our personality, but most importantly, they've helped us tap into the U.S. market. Every night, they seamlessly convert traffic into conversations and conversations into booked meetings for our sales team. It made a new market possible."

The End of Business Development Reps (BDRS)?

In a world where we now have intelligent chatbots that can, as Rich Wood put it, "seamlessly convert traffic into conversations and conversations into booked meetings for our sales team," it begs the question: Do we still need BDRs sitting between Marketing and Sales, serving as an additional "pit stop" for leads who are trying to move through our buying process?

Loren Padelford, the VP and general manager of Shopify Plus, had this to say about the BDR process in a 2015 LinkedIn post: "It's illogical and it's not the way your customers want to interact with your company. . . . This artificial hand-off creates a choppy experience for the customer, which in today's super-fast, next-generation sales environments can actually slow the sales cycle down." And while BDRs have, in the past, been instrumental to the growth of several successful companies, perhaps most famously when they helped fuel Salesforce's growth in the early 2000s, Padelford had this to say to companies that were thinking about trying to replicate that model: "You are not Salesforce and this isn't the early 2000s."

Meanwhile, a 2017 report from The Bridge Group that looked at how many meetings sales reps booked when (a) they did *not* have BDRs working with them and (b) when they *did* have BDRs working with them, found that BDRs didn't really make much difference. As the report's author, David Skok, wrote: "It was expected that results would indicate a large uplift for the latter, but that was not the case." Instead, sales reps who were supported by BDRs reported "only 0.8 more demos per week, on average" compared to those who didn't have BDR support.

Ultimately, in the face of new technology and changing communication preferences, the traditional BDR process has become less effective. As growth specialist Dan Smith wrote on the Sales Hacker blog in 2017, today's BDRs "are tasked to meet the demand of a new kind of buyer that primarily lives online, buys faster, and spends more on cloud services than ever before." Unfortunately, meeting this demand has proven challenging. And making the problem worse is the fact that instead of trying a new approach, most companies have simply doubled down on what they already know. To make up for slipping conversion rates, they've been hiring more BDRs so they can send more annoying emails and make more interruptive calls.

The Problem Is the Process, Not the People

To clarify, the underlying issue here is the BDR process that companies have built and been relying on, not the BDRs themselves. Ultimately, BDRs have what many consider to be the most difficult job in Sales. As Jonathan Vaudreuil, director of Sales Development at Upserve, wrote in a 2016 blog post: "Spending 100% of your time calling, emailing, and cold prospecting is a brutal way to spend all day, every day. You have to deal with the fact that most people don't pick up the phone and that most people who do pick up say 'no.' Almost all of your emails will not be replied to. Most of your replies will be a 'no' as well. Being a BDR is the hardest job in sales because you're doing the dirty work for someone else."

The good news: Today, BDRs can have intelligent chatbots do that "dirty work" instead.

In the past, companies needed BDRs to follow up with the leads that Marketing captured so they could further qualify them before sending them to Sales. And because phone and email (and to a lesser extent, social media) were the only channels available to them, BDRs had no choice but to bombard people with outbound calls and emails. With the rise of messaging and chatbots, however, real-time engagement has become not only possible, but scalable.

Instead of replacing BDRs, chatbots are poised to revolutionize the BDR process. The BDRs of the future will no longer spend all of their time "smiling and dialing" and blasting out emails Instead, they'll be having real-time conversations with website visitors, and chatbots will help them do it.

How Ipswitch Modernized Their BDR Process Using Real-Time Conversations

The BDRs working at the IT management software company Ipswitch had tried using messaging on their website before, but they weren't able to effectively target leads or automate the lead qualification process. As a result, BDRs ended up spending most of their time fielding customer support questions. Meanwhile, none of the conversation data could be synced with their CRM, so they could never really measure messaging's effectiveness.

However, instead of giving up on using real-time conversations to qualify leads, Ipswitch's BDR team upgraded to a conversational marketing and sales platform, which combined messaging and chatbots and synced with their CRM. They began running their new, conversational BDR process in January of 2018, and, within a few weeks, it became the source of their "best leads," according to one Ipswitch BDR. Ipswitch's CMO, Jeanne Hopkins, told the Drift marketing team it was a "no-brainer" to expand their conversational approach to more and more pages of their website given the quality they were seeing. By March, they were running their conversational BDR process in Spanish as well as in English. By April, the results were in:

After switching to conversations, Ipswitch's BDR team had their best quarter in company history. Conversations became their number one source of leads, accounting for 280 of them—85 of which would convert into opportunities. When they compared conversations to their other lead sources, they found that conversations generated 10 times more opportunities than Google AdWords campaigns and four times more opportunities than the events they were running. Overall, conversations accounted for $1 million in new sales pipeline for Ipswitch in those first few months, as well as 11 new customers.

Sharing the Most Important Metric: Revenue

Marketing and sales teams used to speak two completely different languages. While marketers spoke the language of click-throughs, and conversion rates, and cost per lead, salespeople spoke the language of dollars. The reason for this difference: Historically, it's been hard for marketers to measure how their marketing campaigns influence revenue. Today, it's a different story.

While conversational marketing and sales arose out of the need to deliver a better buying experience to customers, a positive side-effect has been that it's helped rally marketing and sales teams (including BDRs) around a single metric: revenue. Because conversational marketing and sales creates a streamlined buying experience, you can keep track of the interactions leads have on your website and trace the trajectories of those leads—from their first conversations to when they convert into customers. That makes it easy for both marketers and salespeople to see how conversations are influencing revenue.

After implementing a conversational approach, your marketing and sales teams will finally be able to speak the same language. And they'll finally be able to get outside of their respective silos and collaborate. Instead of operating independently and pursuing separate goals, marketing and sales teams can now join forces and drive revenue by delivering a seamless buying experience that's powered by real-time conversations.

In Part Two of this book, I'll give you step-by-step instructions on how to create a seamless, real-time buying experience at your own company.

Part II

Getting Started with Conversational Marketing

Chapter 6

Step One: Add Real-Time Messaging to Your Website and Start Capturing More Leads

The first step to adopting a conversational marketing and sales strategy for your business is to make it as easy as possible for potential customers to talk to you. And in a world where billions of people are now using messaging as their default mode of communication, and where 90% of consumers want to be able to use messaging to talk to business (according to a 2016 study by Twilio), that means you need to add messaging to your website.

With messaging, you'll be able to open up a real-time lead generation channel on your website, which can yield you hundreds if not thousands of net new leads. These are the people who are already on your website looking around, but who, until now, have never bothered to engage. Or, perhaps more accurately, we are the ones who have never bothered to engage with them.

As I mentioned in Chapter One, business-to-business (B2B) companies ended up spending a collective $4.6 billion in 2018 trying to drive people to their websites with advertising. They've also dedicated countless resources to creating top-of-the-funnel content and to optimizing search engines and to engaging people on social media...all in the hope that potential customers would visit their websites. But when that plan succeeds, when potential customers *do* visit a B2B company's website, the experience is akin to walking into an empty store. There's no one there to talk to them or answer their questions, just a lead capture form and the promise of a follow-up. As marketers and salespeople, these are the exact moments when we should be engaging with people—while they're already on our websites and clearly interested in learning more.

The good news: This is an easy fix. It's something you can address *today*, without having to mess up your existing marketing and sales stack. Best of all, you can have everything up and running in just a few minutes.

Replace Your Forms or Add a "Second Net" (Don't Worry, It Takes Five Minutes)

Adding real-time messaging to your website is as simple as copying and pasting a snippet of code (which is provided by the messaging service you're using) into your website's source code. It's the same process for installing Google Analytics or any other marketing or sales application, and it doesn't require a ton of technical know-how. Granted, if you don't have access to your website's source code, you'll need to tag in someone on your team who can help. Either way, once that snippet has been added, a messaging widget (see Figure 6.1) will appear on your website and visitors will be able to engage with you in real time. Depending on how much traffic

FIGURE 6.1 Examples of different messaging widget styles.

your website gets, your first conversation with a visitor might begin within a matter of seconds.

To make messaging feel like a native feature of your website, you can customize the color and icon style of your messaging widget so that it aligns with the design of your website. And to ensure that you're deriving as much value from messaging as possible from the get-go, there are several other ways you can fine-tune your setup, from writing the perfect welcome message, to setting online/offline hours, to creating separate messaging inboxes so visitors are always connected to the people at your company who are best-suited to help them. But before we dive into the fine details of how you can fully customize your messaging strategy, there's still an important question that needs answering:

Once you've added messaging to your website, what should you do with your lead capture forms?

The #NoForms Approach to Conversational Marketing and Sales

Of course, if you read Part I of this book, the answer to the "What should I do with my forms?" question probably seems obvious: You should get rid of them.

That's exactly what we did at Drift. We went into our content management system (CMS) and took them off of our landing pages. For our ebook landing pages, we added links that allowed visitors to download the books directly— no forms required. And across every page of our website, we had our messaging widget that allowed visitors to engage with us in real time.

When we'd finished this transformation, there were just two forms left on our website, both of which had a single field for capturing email addresses. The first was on our homepage and allowed people to sign up for our free product (we couldn't really ditch that one) and the second was on our blog and allowed readers to sign up for our newsletter (although we later created a chatbot for managing newsletter signups).

The "Second Net" Approach to Conversational Marketing and Sales

For some companies, however, especially large companies and those that have dozens if not hundreds of landing pages set up that are capturing leads, the prospect of getting rid of all of the forms on those pages may seem, at best, daunting, and at worst, like a crazy gamble. And getting buy-in from the people you need buy-in from in order to make it happen might be impossible. That's something I can completely understand, and that's also why, even though I'm not a big fan of forms myself, I don't think you absolutely have to take them down in order to start seeing the benefits of conversational marketing and sales. Instead, if you can keep using your forms as a first net for capturing leads, you can add messaging to your website as a second net. It's the perfect way to start experimenting with a conversational approach without having to make any changes to your existing setup whatsoever.

Chris Willis, former CMO at Perfecto Mobile (now CMO at Acrolinx), used the "second net" approach on the Perfecto Mobile website. Instead of getting rid of lead capture forms, he started giving visitors the option to chat via messaging as an alternative to filling out those forms (see Figure 6.2).

At the time, Chris's goal was to do a better job of converting visitors into leads on the Perfect Mobile website. As he told the Drift marketing team, "We were sitting at about a 6% conversion of our web traffic, which is about the industry standard. But what we wanted to do was increase the overall conversion rate of traffic because our traffic was pretty good."

Within three months of using messaging as a "second net," the Perfecto Mobile website's conversion rate grew from 6% to nearly 10%. As Chris explained, "We started to see the promise of what we were trying to do, which was to create more out of our base." After six months of using messaging, their conversion rate had grown to 20%.

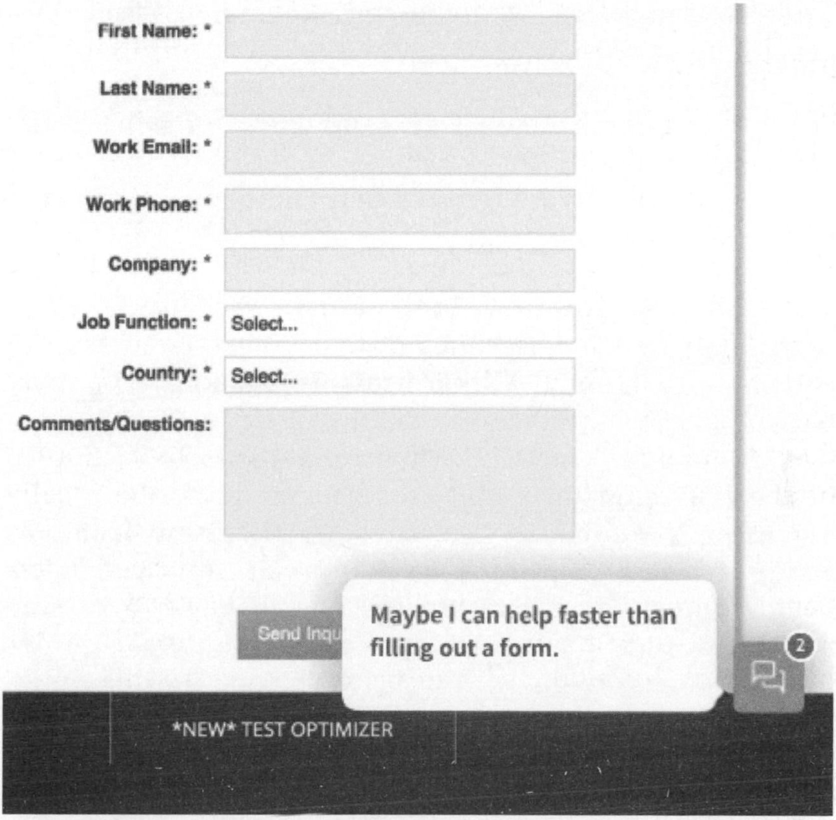

FIGURE 6.2 Messaging offers website visitors a speedier alternative to the traditional lead capture form.

The takeaway here: Whether you become part of the #NoForms movement or use the "second net" approach, you can start using messaging to drive value for your business immediately.

Integrating with the Tools You Already Use

Marketing and sales teams are often hesitant to switch over to new software tools. After all, new tools require training and ramp-up time and can disrupt the processes that teams have painstakingly instituted and optimized over the years. But when it comes to adding messaging to your website, there's no need to fret: By integrating it with all of the tools you're already using, you can start having real-time conversations—and start seeing how those conversations are affecting your business's bottom line—without having to adapt to an entirely new system (and without having to disrupt your old one).

Here are four types of tools that companies commonly integrate with messaging:

1. Team Collaboration Tools (such as Slack). With more than 70,000 companies now paying for the service, and more than eight million users accessing it on a daily basis, Slack has become the default internal communication channel for a large chunk of the B2B world. And most of the B2B companies that aren't using Slack specifically are using a similar service, such as Microsoft Teams or Stride (formerly HipChat). So many marketers and salespeople already have a messaging portal they're accessing daily. Instead of having to access a second portal in order to have conversations with website visitors, they can integrate the two services and respond to website visitors from directly within Slack (or whatever collaboration tool they're using). That way there's no learning curve or ramp-up time.

2. CRMs (such as Salesforce). After integrating messaging with a customer relationship management (CRM) system, new contact records can be created automatically for leads you generate through messaging, and attributes, such as their names and the names of the companies they work at, can be mapped into those records automatically. You'll also have the option of being able to add transcripts from your messaging conversations to the corresponding contact records in your CRM. By integrating messaging with a CRM, you're able to plug a new source of leads into your marketing and sales stack and show everyone the value without having to change any of the structures or workflows you've already built.

3. Marketing Automation Tools (such as HubSpot and Marketo). Chances are if your company has historically been using forms to capture leads, you've probably been funneling those leads into a marketing automation tool such as HubSpot or Marketo. These tools make it easy for you to follow up with new leads via automated emails. And while at Drift we have a slightly different approach to email marketing, which you'll learn all about in the next chapter, being able to connect messaging with automation tools is still going to be essential for many companies. As was the case with CRMs, these types of integrations allow new contact records to be created for leads that come in through messaging, as well as for attributes to be mapped over. The conversations you have, meanwhile, are logged as activities in your contacts' timelines, allowing you to see exactly how messaging factors into your marketing mix and influences deals.

4. Analytics Tools (such as Google Analytics). Just as marketers and salespeople value being able to have conversations with coworkers *and* potential customers in a single, centralized place (such as Slack), they also value being able to review their performance metrics in a single, centralized place. By integrating messaging with an existing analytics tool, such as Google Analytics, you can start reviewing the performance of messaging alongside the performance of the channels you've already been measuring. Specifically, the integration could allow you to track how many new conversations you're starting via messaging, how many emails you're capturing via messaging, as well as how many sales meetings you're booking via messaging. And you could track all of these new metrics from the comfort of the analytics tool you've already been using.

Put Up a Welcome Message

Once you have the bones of your real-time lead generation channel in place (by which I mean you've installed messaging and integrated with all the tools you're already using), you can start fleshing out the experience. And one of your first steps should be to put up a welcome message (see Figure 6.3).

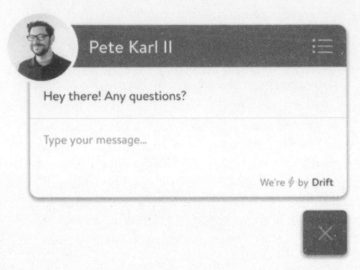

FIGURE 6.3 An example of a welcome message on the Drift website.

A welcome message is a short message that pops up in the corner of your website (out of your messaging widget) and automatically greets your website visitors. It's how you let people know that your website is open for business and that you have employees on standby, ready to answer any questions people might have.

For websites that have low volumes of traffic, it's best to have your welcome message appear on every page. That way you never miss a chance to engage with potential customers. For websites that receive high volumes of traffic, however, you may want to have your welcome message appear only for certain types of visitors, like those who live in the countries your company caters to, or only on certain pages, like your pricing page. That way you can filter out visitors who are unlikely to buy. We'll explore targeting and filtering in-depth in Chapter Nine, but for now, let's turn our attention to a more pressing matter: what you should be saying in your welcome message.

How to Write an Effective Welcome Message

As the first message a visitor sees on your website, a welcome message should grab the attention of your visitors and encourage them to engage with you. Now, on one hand, writing a message like that is pretty easy. You can simply put something like, "Welcome! We'll give you a $1,000 if you respond to this message and start a conversation with us." But, as you'd soon discover, that's not a very sustainable model. So I recommend following these three guidelines instead:

1. **Ask a question.** Don't use your welcome message to make a passive statement ("Hello, we are x company and we sell y and z"), use it to ask a question. Even if it's something as simple as "How can we help you?" or "What brought you here today?" a question is always the better option when you're trying to elicit a response.

2. **Be succinct.** One of the biggest benefits of using messaging is its speed. As a potential customer, you can have your questions answered in real time, and as marketer or salesperson, you can help that potential customer move through your funnel more quickly. But here's the thing: if you write a welcome message that's two paragraphs long, you're going to end up slowing people down, assuming anyone even bothers to read it. So for best results, you need to keep that message short and sweet. Say hello, ask a question, and start the conversation.

3. **Have fun with it.** Part of what made the first wave of messaging or "live chat" for business websites so lackluster was that everything was too programmatic. Back then, every company using messaging stuck to the same formal tone, and the overall experience felt cold and robotic. As marketers and salespeople, that's not what we should be striving for. By injecting a little humor and fun into your welcome message, you can stir up interest and get people talking. Case in point: There's a pet subscription service company that saw their messaging engagement skyrocket after setting up a welcome message that asks visitors what their pets' names are.

Set Expectations with Online/ Offline Hours

Welcome messages are designed to appear on your website when your team is online and available to chat. Of course, that's not always going to be the case. Marketers and salespeople need to sleep, and unless you set up a chatbot (which you'll learn how to do in Chapter Ten), managing messaging 24 hours a day can be a struggle, especially for smaller companies. That's why it's important to establish online and offline hours when using messaging—so you can make it clear to visitors when you're available to chat and when you're not.

For example, you may decide to set your online hours as 9 a.m. to 5 p.m., Monday through Friday. During those online hours, you can have your welcome message appear as usual and engage with visitors in real time. But during your offline hours, before 9 a.m. or after 5 p.m., or anytime over the weekend, you can have an away message appear (see Figure 6.4). You can also manually toggle between online and offline mode as needed, allowing you to display your

FIGURE 6.4 An example of an away message on the Drift website.

away message during times when you need to be offline, like when you're having a team-wide meeting.

Ideally, of course, you'd be able to have conversations around the clock, but the next best thing is being open and honest with potential customers about your availability (as opposed to leaving them in the dark). That's where the away message comes into play.

How to Write an Effective Away Message

In addition to letting your visitors know that your team is currently unavailable to chat, your away message can set expectations for visitors (by letting them know when you'll be back online) and can prompt visitors to leave their email addresses so you can connect with them later. Here are three key points to remember when crafting your away message:

1. **Be Honest.** If you're going to be offline for a 12-hour stretch, don't tell your visitors someone will respond within a few minutes. Because guess what? When those visitors stick around for a few minutes and no one responds, they'll feel ignored, and that doesn't make for a great experience. Your away message should set expectations for visitors, not deceive them.

2. **Encourage visitors to leave a message.** Even when you're offline, you can still use messaging to drive engagement. In your away message, you should encourage visitors to leave you a note so that as soon as you're back online, you can answer their questions and/or provide whatever help they need.

3. **Don't forget to ask for an email address.** In some cases, the visitors who reply to your away message might not return to your website to continue the conversation over messaging. That's why it's important to ask for an email address: so you can follow up with them directly if needed.

Show Your Face

Ask any of our designers at Drift and they'll tell you: I have a bit of an obsession with using faces in everything we do. Whether it's our product, the homepage of our website, or the images on our blog, I have found faces to be crucial when it comes to humanizing our brand and humanizing the customer experience. So instead of relying on stock images or cartoons, we've been taking our own photos around the office, at the offices we visit, and at team outings and conferences. That way, we can use photos of our actual employees and customers in our marketing and have their faces represent our brand. This helps us make stronger connections with our existing customers as well as with our potential customers.

Turns out, there's a scientific reason for why faces are so powerful. As biologist Nathan H. Lents, Ph.D., explained in *Psychology Today* in 2017, faces play a crucial role in human communication, starting when we're infants. To quote Lents: "The face is the means by which we send and receive communication long before words or even gestures, and this communication is more precise and nuanced than clumsy cries and grunts." He went on to explain that humans have more diversity in our facial features than other species and that we also look at each other's faces more frequently compared to other species, especially during communication. Lents's conclusion: "Our faces were key to our individuality, our communication, and our connection to other people. In other words, our faces were, and still are, a central aspect of our sociality."

Using Faces to Make Messaging a More Trustworthy Channel

When it comes to using messaging for conversational marketing and sales, faces are a must. Marketers and salespeople who are going to be using messaging to engage with potential customers should upload photos of themselves, in addition to including their full names. By displaying real faces and real names, you can help show potential customers that the "chat agents" they're talking to are actual people—not anonymous corporate entities.

That was part of the problem with the first wave of messaging back in the 1990s: Website visitors didn't always trust

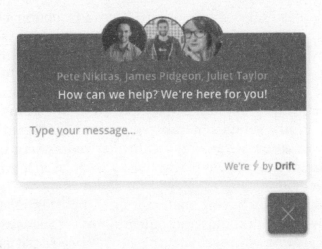

FIGURE 6.5 A welcome message on the Drift website that's displaying multiple faces.

the answers they were receiving, as it was unclear who they were hearing them from. Today, you can have the photo of the employee who is currently managing messaging appear automatically as part of your welcome message. And if you have multiple employees using messaging on your website at the same time, you can have multiple faces appear (see Figure 6.5). In addition to helping set expectations for visitors so they have a sense of who they'll be talking to, displaying a bunch of smiling faces on your website is also a welcoming gesture.

Think about it: If your website was a store and people walked in, you wouldn't hide behind the counter—you'd smile and say hello. And that's exactly what we should be doing on our websites.

Create Separate Inboxes for Sales, Support, Success, Etc.

While adding messaging to your website creates a real-time lead generation channel, it simultaneously creates a real-time communication channel that anyone—including existing customers—can use to get in touch with your business. While this is absolutely a positive and is something we'll explore more in the second half of the book, having your paying customers, free users (if you offer a free product), *and* new visitors all reaching out on messaging at the same time asking different types of questions makes it hard for marketers and salespeople to focus their efforts.

The solution: Create separate messaging inboxes that are managed by different teams and that cater to different groups of people. For example, you could create a Customer Success inbox for paying customers, a Support inbox for free users, and a Marketing and Sales inbox for leads. For the person visiting your website, the experience remains seamless, but behind the scenes, the conversation can be routed to the team that is best-suited to help. For example, let's say during a Support conversation, it becomes clear that a free user is interested in upgrading to a paid plan. With a few clicks, Support can route that user to the Sales inbox, where a sales rep will be waiting.

Instead of having a single team manage every single conversation that happens on your website, by setting up separate inboxes you can divide the load and allow teams to hone in on providing the best experience possible to the people they're best-equipped to help.

Let Chatbots Lend a Hand

One of the best ways to figure out which inbox a conversation should be routed to is simply to ask: "Who would you like to talk to today? Sales? Support?" And while this is a job that humans are certainly capable of, it can get a bit repetitive. That's why at Drift, one of the first chatbots we ever built was one that asked our website visitors which team they wanted to get in contact with, and then routed them there accordingly (see Figure 6.6).

Automating the lead routing process with chatbots makes it easier for buyers to move through your sales funnel more quickly. It's like a fast lane: Instead of buyers having to slow down and wait for the company to decide whether

FIGURE 6.6 Using a chatbot to route leads to the right departments.

they're qualified enough to talk to a sales rep, today's buyers can make that decision on their own and be connected to a sales rep in real time.

Know Your Stuff (and Use Tools That Can Help)

Once you have all of your integrations in place, you've written the perfect welcome message, and you have your inboxes set up the way you want them, you're inevitably going to have to take the logical next step: actually talking to people.

So far in this chapter, we've focused on the different ways you can configure messaging on your website to ensure you're set up for conversational marketing and sales success. Now we're going to focus on how you can prepare for the actual, one-to-one conversations you'll be having. And really, what it all boils down to is that you need to know your stuff.

Brace Yourself: Questions Are Coming

Once you have messaging up and running on your website, your website visitors will start asking questions. And as we discovered at Drift, after a few days or weeks, you'll begin to hear the same questions being asked over and over and over. These can include questions about using your product and its different features, as well as questions about pricing and—for companies that use tiered pricing—what's included in your different plans.

There's no doubt that these questions are super valuable for your business, as they can help you identify gaps in your product offerings as well as gaps in your marketing. But in order to provide a positive experience for the people asking those questions, you need to be able to answer them.

In addition to studying the ins and outs of your product during your offline hours, there are a few best practices you can follow to ensure you always have the answers.

1. **Create saved replies.** For the questions you hear over and over and over, you can write and save canned responses that anyone on your team can paste into conversations. These saved replies can help your team answer common questions with consistency. However, to avoid conversations sounding robotic, I recommend that marketers and salespeople never use saved replies word-for-word. Instead, you should always tweak them to match the way you personally write and communicate.

2. **Keep your company's help desk open when chatting with visitors.** A lot of the questions people end up asking on your website are questions that they could ultimately find the answers to themselves in your company's knowledge base or help desk. But see, that's why those visitors are starting a conversation with you via messaging in the first place: They don't want to go searching for the answers, they'd rather just ask someone and have the searching done for them. (That's where you come in.)

3. **Integrate with your help desk and let chatbots do the work.** Of course, with the rise of chatbots, the humans at your company are no longer the only ones who can answer questions via messaging. By integrating your company's help desk

FIGURE 6.7 A chatbot suggesting help docs based on a user's question.

or knowledge base and setting up a chatbot (see Figure 6.7), you can automate the process of looking up help desk answers. You can then have the chatbot share links to the specific help docs where visitors can find those answers.

One of the ways you can use this type of chatbot is to have it jump in during times when you're online but there's an influx of visitors. You can also have it run during offline hours so visitors can find answers to basic questions at any time, day or night.

Capture Leads (Without Using Lead Forms)

Once you have the basic setup for conversational marketing and sales in place on your website, you'll no longer have to rely on forms in order to capture leads. Instead, you'll be able to use messaging as a net new source of leads, and you'll be able to capture those leads 24 hours a day.

Even when you're offline, you can configure messaging so that it's always adding value and always responding to new leads in real time—things a lead capture form will never be able to do. With messaging on your website, you'll be able to capture leads using conversations. What's more, you'll be able to qualify leads using conversations as well.

But before we turn our attention to the art (and science) of qualifying leads via messaging, I want to spend the next chapter exploring how we can revamp an older mode of communication—a mode of communication we're all familiar with—and bring it into the real-time world we now live in.

Chapter 7

Step Two: Give Your Email Marketing Strategy a Real-Time Makeover

There's no beating around the bush here: Email just isn't the channel it used to be. As we've already explored, today's buyers—millennial buyers in particular—are using email less and less and turning to messaging more and more.

Arguably, the downfall of email as a communication channel began just a few years after it was invented in the early 1970s, when, in 1978, a marketing manager working at a computer company sent out the world's first spam email. This was back before we had even started calling spam emails "spam." The unsolicited email, which was blasted out to 400 of the 2,600 people using ARPANET (an early version of the internet), advertised the company's new line of mainframe computers. It also set the tone for how marketing teams would use email in the years to follow.

Flash forward to 2004, and PCMag.com is publishing an editorial titled "The Death of E-Mail," in which the columnist writes: "It's quite possible that spam alone is killing e-mail." A slew of similarly themed articles will appear in the years to follow, with headlines including "5 Scientific

Reasons Why Email Is the Absolute Worst" (*Mic*, 2014) and "How Email Became the Most Reviled Communication Experience Ever" (*Fast Company*, 2015).

And while people have been predicting email's demise for decades, the reality is that it's still alive and kicking. For proof, just ask yourself this question: Did you check your email today?

Email Isn't Dead (You're Just Doing It Wrong)

While it's no longer the world's most popular communication channel, email is still being used by billions of people. In fact, there are now more than 3.8 billion email users worldwide, according to a 2018 study by Radicati Group. For comparison, there were just 1.9 billion email users back in 2009.

As marketers and salespeople, we can't afford to ignore email as a channel. Even though messaging (and chatbots) now offer a real-time alternative, there are still times when it makes sense to use email in order to start or rekindle conversations. And while some companies have been nervously watching as their email open rates creep lower and lower, and, as a result, have been deriding email as a broken, ineffective channel, the underlying issue isn't that email as a channel is broken—it's that the way we've been using email is broken. Here's how Drift's VP of Growth, Guillaume Cabane, explained it on an episode of Seeking Wisdom (the podcast I co-host with Drift's head of marketing):

> *The thing that's important is that it's not the channel that's broken in most cases, it's the tool that's broken. When we think of all those channels—chat, email, the web—often we marketers have broken the relationship with the customer. But the channel itself is still valid. If someone comes to me and says, "Email isn't working for me, the web isn't working for me," I say, "Get out of here. Email is working great, you're just not using it right."*

Why Do Cold Emails and Phishing Attacks Have Similar Success Rates?

Just so we're clear on the terminology: Cold emails are unsolicited emails that marketers and salespeople send to potential customers with the hope that they'll reply and, of course, eventually buy. Phishing attacks, meanwhile, are when cyber-criminals attempt to trick people into giving away sensitive information (like passwords) by sending emails that appear to from legitimate sources. According to Guillaume, the average success rate for these types of attacks is around 0.1%. Meanwhile, the average response rate for a cold email is about 1%—better than the success rate of a phishing attack, but not by much. And for marketers and salespeople, Guillaume thinks that should be a red flag. As he explained:

> It's in the same range, and the crazy thing is that you can think of the person who does the scam as a marketer. They're trying to convince the other person that the message is legit and that the product is good. . . . The reason why I like to compare them is to prove that in both cases, those are awful experiences. If you have a 1% conversion rate on your email, it means that you're annoying 99 people, real people, to be able to sell your product to one person. And that's pretty close to spam. That's awful.

The Problems with Traditional Email Marketing

So how did email marketing become such an awful experience for buyers and such a low-performing channel for companies? I've identified three key factors.

1. Email Isn't Real-Time

While there are plenty of studies that have looked at the best days—and times of day—to send emails, the reality is

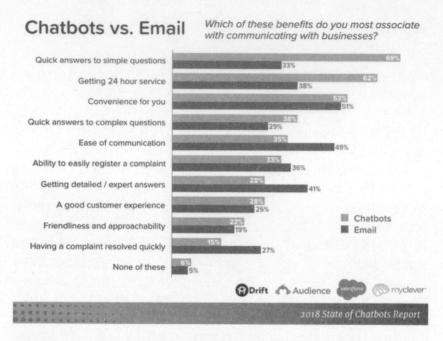

Chatbots vs. Email

Which of these benefits do you most associate with communicating with businesses?

Benefit	Chatbots	Email
Quick answers to simple questions	69%	33%
Getting 24 hour service	62%	38%
Convenience for you	53%	51%
Quick answers to complex questions	38%	29%
Ease of communication	35%	49%
Ability to easily register a complaint	33%	36%
Getting detailed / expert answers	28%	41%
A good customer experience	28%	25%
Friendliness and approachability	22%	19%
Having a complaint resolved quickly	15%	27%
None of these	6%	5%

🟦 Chatbots
⬛ Email

⊕ Drift 🔺 Audience ☁ salesforce 🧠 myclever

2018 State of Chatbots Report

FIGURE 7.1 When it comes to getting speedy responses, consumers prefer chatbots over email.

that the best time to get in touch with potential customers is always the same: it's when *they* want to get in touch. That's why messaging and chatbots have been growing in popularity. As we discovered in a 2018 report that we published at Drift (in collaboration with SurveyMonkey Audience, Salesforce, and myclever), consumers ranked chatbots significantly higher than email when it came to both getting quick answers to simple questions (69% versus 33%) and getting 24-hour service (62% versus 38%). See Figure 7.1 for the full breakdown.

With traditional email, it's impossible to give today's buyers the type of real-time, on-demand experience that they've come to expect—thanks in no small part to the rise of messaging and chatbots. While email is a familiar channel and a channel that's great for giving in-depth answers to complex questions, it just hasn't been fast enough to keep up with the pace of today's buyers.

2. Email Is Abused

Yes, this is an obvious one, but it's something that we all need to drill into our heads: As marketers and sales-people, we've been sending way, way too many emails. Instead of using email as a channel for having one-to-one conversations with people who are likely to buy, we've been using it as a speakerphone for blasting out our content and our promotions to as many people as possible. Instead of focusing on the experience we are providing, we've been focusing almost exclusively on the numbers, obsessing over open rates and click-through rates. And when it comes to increasing those numbers, the solution has always been the same: send more emails and hope for the best.

Using this "spray and pray" approach to email marketing, we've not only been abusing email as a communication channel, but we've also been abusing the email inboxes of our potential customers.

3. Email Isn't Smart

It's an all-too-common scenario: Multiple people at your company all sending emails to the same potential customer, sometimes on the same day. For example, imagine a sales rep sends a one-to-one email to a potential customer, offering to help out and answer any questions that he or she might have. Then an hour later, your marketing team sends an email inviting that same potential customer to a webinar. And then an hour after *that* email goes out, your product team sends that potential customer a product update email.

On the one hand, there's some clear over-communicating happening here, as the emails companies are sending are piling up in people's inboxes. On the other hand, there's a lack of communication internally. In a perfect world, or at a perfect company, I should say, teams would be perfectly in sync with all of the emails they're sending. But once team sizes start to grow and your company's headcount balloons from dozens, to hundreds, to thousands, coordinating all of those emails becomes nearly impossible. So instead of having to rely on people and internal processes to ensure we're not over-sending emails, why can't we rely on the communication channel itself? The answer: Until recently, email hasn't been smart. Traditional marketing automation technology was designed to maximize results for your marketing team, not optimize the experience for your potential customers.

A Few Simple Tweaks for Bringing Your Email Marketing Strategy into the Real-Time World

To recap, three of the main problems with traditional email marketing have been as follows:

1. Email isn't real-time.
2. Email is abused.
3. Email isn't smart.

The silver lining: With a few simple tweaks, you can modernize your email marketing strategy and start using email as a tool for engaging (and re-engaging) potential customers in real-time conversation. Here's how you do it.

1. Connect Email to Real-Time Messaging

Let's start with the simplest (but also most impactful) change first. In every email you send, start including a hyperlink that allows the recipient to start a real-time conversation with a single click. You can create this hyperlink in seconds inside of your conversational marketing and sales platform. In addition to creating links that trigger conversations with sales reps or other humans at your company, you can also set up links that trigger chatbot conversations. (For example, at Drift, we use the link drift.com/#getademo to trigger a chatbot that lets potential customers book demos with our sales reps.)

From an experience perspective, connecting real-time messaging to email allows buyers to skip the "nurturing" portion of the buying process and proceed directly to having a one-on-one conversation. By simply clicking a link, a buyer can get a direct line to a sales rep (or a sales rep's calendar). What's more, as marketers and salespeople, we can personalize the experiences of people who are starting real-time conversations from our emails. Specifically, we can customize the welcome messages they see, either by calling them out by name and/or referencing the email they were just reading (see Figure 7.2).

After connecting email with real-time time messaging, you'll be able to close the loop between the conversations happening over email and the conversations happening on your website, which in turn will contribute to a more cohesive experience for buyers.

FIGURE 7.2 A welcome message on the Drift website, personalized for someone who we're also communicating with via email.

2. Send Fewer (More Highly Targeted) Emails

The "spray and pray" approach to email marketing is both inefficient and—for a lot of teams—producing diminishing returns. The solution: Stop going broad and start going narrow. Instead of flooding inboxes with emails that share as much information as possible with the hope that something will resonate, start honing your message to address the specific concerns of the people you're emailing.

As Drift's VP of Growth Guillaume explained (during that same episode of Seeking Wisdom I mentioned earlier), not all marketing and sales teams are seeing that dreadful 1% cold email response rate he cited. Some teams are actually seeing much, much higher results. Their secret? Being relevant. To quote Guillaume:

> If you look at the other end, people who create really good experiences, people who know how to use that channel, they get 15 to 20% response rates—positive response rates. I've seen a company that has 44% response rates to their outbound emails, their cold emails. And it's not because they've spent more time, it's because their message is more relevant. It's the relevance of the message. There's value in reading that message. It's valuable to the person who receives it. It tells you where that buried treasure is that's buried in your garden.

That "buried treasure" is the value a potential customer is missing out on. It's the solution to the specific problem he or she is trying to solve. So as marketers and salespeople, in order for our emails to resonate, we need to be giving our potential customers personalized "treasure maps."

Instead of using email to list off every benefit our product or service can provide, we should be using it to talk about the *one* benefit that a particular buyer is most interested in learning more about. And if this a buyer who has already had a conversation on your website, good news: You can review the conversation transcript to easily figure out what that one thing is. If the person you're emailing hasn't had a conversation with you yet, you can figure out what benefit to highlight by looking at the industry he or she is in, the number of employees at his or her company, and other attributes. And when writing your email, you could—for example—mention similar companies that are already customers of yours and share what made those customers decide to buy.

3. Use Smart Filters

While connecting email to real-time messaging and sending fewer, more highly targeted emails will definitely help contribute to a better email marketing experience for buyers, those actions alone can't solve everything. More specifically, there's still that annoying issue of buyers being sent multiple emails from multiple teams.

The solution: When setting up our email audience lists, we need to start using "smart filters," filters that look at a person's behavior across both email and messaging and can automatically skip over contacts you've recently engaged with (or you're engaging with in real time). With a single click, you can apply a smart filter and ensure that potential customers aren't being inundated with emails.

Ultimately, we need to start conversations with our potential customers where they are. So if they're on our websites, that's where we should be engaging them, using messaging. And, thanks to smart filters, we can ensure that during those messaging conversations, we won't be sending them emails at the same time. That way we can keep our potential customers' attention focused on the conversation at hand. However, if we see that potential customers have left our websites and haven't been back for a while, we can switch over to email in order to reach out and try to bring them back.

4. Send Plain Text Emails

At Drift, even before we made the decision to get rid of lead forms and ungate our content, we decided to get rid of designed HTML emails and have our marketing and sales teams only send plain text emails instead. A quick definition: Plain text emails are exactly what they sound like. They look just like the emails you send to your friends and family. There are no fancy design elements, just the words and images (and emojis) you want to share.

As was the case with switching from forms to messaging, switching from HTML emails to plain text emails was at odds with what the traditional marketing and sales playbook recommended. Just look at the emails you receive from most companies today. There are big blocks of color, intricate typefaces, logos . . . they almost feel like flyers or advertisements you'd get in the mail. But think about it for a second: What do most of us do when we find flyers or advertisements in our mailboxes? Exactly: We toss them in the recycling bin. Meanwhile, what are the types of letters most of us always open, often immediately? Letters that appear to be from friends or family members.

Direct response marketer and copywriter Gary C. Halbert explained this phenomenon in his book *The Boron Letters* (2013). To quote Halbert:

> *It is my contention that everybody divides their mail every day into two piles. An "A-Pile" and a "B-Pile." The "A" pile contains letters that appear to be personal. Like letters from friends, relatives, business associates, and so on. On the other hand, the "B" pile contains those envelopes that, like the example above, obviously, contain a commercial message. Now, here's the way it works: Everybody always opens all of their "A" pile mail. And, for obvious reasons. After all, everybody wants to read their personal mail.*

By using plain text emails, you can replicate the feeling or vibe of a personal letter, thus increasing the likelihood of getting those emails into people's "A" piles. Even if you're using marketing automation to send them, emails composed in plain text still look more authentic than their designed, flyer-like counterparts. Granted, looks aren't the most important factor in this equation: your copy is—the words you're writing. But if you eliminate unnecessary design elements from your emails, readers will be able to focus exclusively on the information you're sharing and the value you're conveying. With plain text emails, you're making it clear to potential customers that you're not trying to overload their senses or dazzle them, you're trying to help them.

Why Replies Are the Most Important Email Metric

At Drift, one of the first marketing emails we converted into plain text was our welcome email for new newsletter subscribers, which we send out automatically to people who sign up for our newsletter. We recognized right away that the plain text format aligned perfectly with the friendly, familiar tone our head of marketing, Dave Gerhardt, was using in his email copy. And as soon as we made the switch, we saw immediate proof that this approach was working: People, hundreds of people, were replying. And no, they weren't replying to ask to be unsubscribed from our email list; many of them were actually just commenting on how much they liked the email itself.

That's when it dawned on us: Doing email marketing the right way means having an actual conversation. It's not just about what you have to tell people, it's about what you can learn from them. So we decided to update our welcome email even further to make it more explicit that we wanted people to respond (see Figure 7.3). Today, that email has a response rate of around 30%.

Given the volume of marketing emails that people receive each and every day, the fact that someone would go out of his or her way and take the time to reply to your email is significant, and it's a sign that your message is resonating. That's why I consider replies to be the most important email metric we can track. At Drift, we include email replies in our reporting dashboard and monitor it alongside how many messaging conversations or "chats" we're generating through email, as well as how many sales meetings we're booking. (Note: We'll learn more about using email to schedule sales meetings in Chapter Thirteen.)

OK let's get this out of the way.

Even though this is an automated email...

I just wanted to say hey and let you know that I'm a real person.

I'm Dave and I work on the marketing team here at Drift. I might not know you personally yet, but I'm pumped that you're here.

You have my word that we'll be respectful of your inbox and only email you when we have some fresh new content (or something that is worth telling you about).

One favor before I go: reply to this email and let me know why you signed up?

Would love to learn more about you.

Talk soon.

- Dave

Director of Marketing, Drift.com

FIGURE 7.3 The plain text email we send to new newsletter subscribers at Drift.

Where Open Rates and Click-Through Rates Fall Down

The traditional email marketing playbook taught us to optimize for two main metrics: open rates, or the percentage of people opening our emails, and click-through rates, or the percentage of people who are clicking on the links inside of our emails. Of course, as a marketing team, these are logical things to measure. After all, every team wants to know how many people are taking the time to look at and engage with the emails they're sending. But as a result of focusing almost exclusively on those two metrics, we've been ignoring the fact that email is a two-way communication channel.

While analyzing open rates and click-through rates can teach us something about our potential customers, having one-to-one conversations with those potential customers can teach us more.

That's why the overarching goal of email marketing shouldn't be to reach as many people as possible or to get as many people as possible to visit a landing page, it should be to get people to reply, and to have actual conversations with us. That's because, ultimately, every sale starts with a relationship, and every relationship starts with a conversation.

In the next chapter, we'll explore how you can master the art (and science) of having those conversations.

Chapter 8

Step Three: Master the Art (and Science) of Qualifying Leads Through Conversation

While adding real-time messaging to your website (as well as to your emails) will allow your marketing and sales teams to start having more conversations, technology alone can't guarantee that those conversations will result in new leads and customers for your business. Adapting to a conversational marketing and sales strategy isn't just about using the right tools, it's about asking the right questions and using conversations to build relationships. As a marketer or salesperson who's interested in adopting a conversational strategy, that means you're going to need to work on your conversational skills.

The good news: Even for those who are not natural conversationalists, there is a science to using conversations in order to elicit the right information so you can qualify a lead. But at the same time, there's an art to it as well. Because if everyone at your company robotically followed the same conversation protocol, instead of being themselves and letting their personalities shine through, the overall experience would suffer.

For the past several decades, companies and their buyers have been drifting apart. Their relationships have been strained. By adopting a friendly tone and talking to your potential customers as if you were talking to a trusted friend (and not just to "some lead"), you'll be able to help repair those relationships, one conversation at a time.

Of course, that's easier said than done. And one of the things I've seen companies stumble on time and time again: figuring out what to say to the people they're talking to.

So, Uh, What Do I Say?

First things first: Say "Hi," or "Hello," or "Hey there." However you want to greet your potential customers, make sure you do it *and* that you do it right away—as soon as someone clicks on the welcome message on your website (or clicks a link in an email you sent) and starts a conversation. Even if you're chatting with another potential customer at the time, it's important to greet new people immediately. That way they know there's actually someone there. Also, if you're going to need a minute to wrap up a previous conversation before you can help someone, be honest about it and tell that person upfront: "Hey there! I'll be with you in just a minute." Trust me: It's better to engage right away and set expectations rather than to leave someone hanging. As a conversational marketer or salesperson, the last thing you want to see is a potential customer typing, "Hello? Hello? Hello? Is anybody there?"

When you think about it, all you're doing here is the same thing employees do at a brick-and-mortar store. Even if there's one person running the place, that person will greet every new customer who walks in the door. Ultimately, whether someone's taking the time to visit your store or to visit your website, he or she is worthy of a "Hello."

Let Them Know You're Human

If you're using chatbots to welcome website visitors and to route them to the right teams, you can also use your opening greeting as an opportunity to establish that you are a human—not a chatbot. For example, after a chatbot routes a new lead your way, you could open by saying something like: "Hey there! Real human here, happy to help." As a marketer or sales rep, it's a great way to break the ice and to make it immediately clear that the chatbot did its job and has now gotten out of the way.

Of course, instead of coming right out and saying it—"I am human!"—you can show off your humanity in other ways. For example, after saying "Hello," you can give a brief overview of who you are and what you do. For me, this might look something like: "Hey, David here, CEO at Drift. How can I help you?"

Ask Questions

Regardless of how you introduce yourself, the most important thing is that after you do it, you should immediately steer the conversation *away* from you and your company and whatever you're selling and *toward* the person you're talking to and the problem he or she is trying to solve. As Dale Carnegie wrote in his now-legendary book, *How to Win Friends and Influence People* (1936): "Talk to someone about themselves and they'll listen for hours."

And what's the best way to get people to talk about themselves? You ask good questions and you pay attention to the answers. As Carnegie wrote, "If you aspire to be a good conversationalist, be an attentive listener. To be interesting, be interested. Ask questions that other persons will enjoy answering." And while in this context Carnegie is writing about using the power of asking questions to win friends, marketing and sales teams can use the same approach to win customers. The only tricky part: coming up with questions that your potential customers will enjoy answering.

The Best Questions to Ask Your Website Visitors

There's one key difference between good questions and bad questions: Value. Good questions generate value for both you *and* for the person you're talking with, while bad questions generate value, at best, just for you, and at worst, for nobody.

Here are a few tips for making sure your qualifying questions are always adding value for both parties:

- **Avoid asking closed questions.** Closed questions are questions that have a simple yes or no answer. When used excessively, they can make conversations feel robotic, as if you're just going down a checklist. By keeping questions open-ended, you allow potential customers to share opinions and insights that might otherwise go unsaid. So, for example, instead of asking a closed question such as, "Do you like using solution X?", to make it open-ended you could ask, "What is it about solution X that you like?"

- **Avoid following a script.** While a script can serve as a backbone for what you say to potential customers, it shouldn't be something that you follow line-by-line and read verbatim. Yes, it's always useful to have a list of proven value-driving questions that you can reference during conversations (we'll look at that in a second), but in order to ensure the best experience possible, you need to let each conversation unfold naturally. Inevitably, some leads are going to take longer to qualify than others. Instead of forcing your script on them and making them adapt, you need to be flexible and learn how to adapt to them.

- **Be authentic.** Most of us have dealt with an over-excited sales rep before; someone who seems way too eager and who panders to us way too much. In the world of conversational marketing and sales, this can take the form of a marketer or sales rep using excessive exclamation marks and/or continually replying "Awesome!" or "Amazing!" to every answer a potential customer gives. So whenever *you* are having a conversation with a potential customer, make sure you're being authentic and that you're not simply saying what you think the person wants to hear.

Now that we've established a few ground rules, let's look at some actual questions you can use for qualifying leads.

A List of Common Qualifying Questions

Of course, the specific qualifying questions you ask your website visitors are going to depend on a variety of factors, from the industry you're in, to the product or service you're selling, to the types of customers you're selling to. But as a general rule, after you have greeted someone and have established that you are an actual, living, breathing person, the following questions can help you figure out whether the person you're talking to is a good fit to buy. At Drift, we use these questions (and variations of them) on a daily basis when chatting with potential customers.

- **"What brought you here today?"** This is one of the first questions you should ask, because the sooner you can figure out why someone has taken the time to visit your website and engage with you, the sooner you can help them on the person on his or her journey and steer the person in the right direction.

- **"Why'd you decide to sign up?"** If you work at a software-as-a-service (SaaS) company and are talking to someone who recently signed up for a free version of your product, you can use this question as an alternative to the "What brought you here today?" question. By pinpointing the reason behind why someone decided to try your free product, you can better evaluate whether or not that person would eventually be a good fit for a paid version of your product.

- **"What are you hoping to accomplish?"** Understanding the aspirations of your potential customers and how they're planning on using your product is crucial to figuring whether or not they'd be a good fit to buy. In some cases, you might discover right away that someone is clearly *not* a good fit based on his or her answer to this question. For example, you might discover that a person is planning on using your product to solve problem X, even though your product was designed specifically to solve problem Y. By asking this question early on in the lead qualification process, you can figure out whether someone's expectations align with what your product actually offers and can ensure no one's time is wasted.

- **"What specific goals are you trying to hit?"** A natural follow-up to "What are you hoping to accomplish?" this question digs deeper into the specifics of how someone is thinking about using your product or service. What metrics is he or she trying to optimize for? How big of an increase (or decrease, depending on the metric) is he or she hoping to see? By understanding the nuances of what a potential customer is expecting, you'll be better-equipped to personalize the buying experience and to tailor your pitch to show how your product or service can add value in the right places.

- **"What tools/products/services are you currently using to hit these goals?"** If the person you're talking to is currently using a competitor's product or service, that's definitely something you'll want to (a) know about and (b) talk about during your conversation. Even if that person isn't using a competing product or service, understanding how that person currently solves (or tries to solve) the problem he or she has will give you insight into how your solution could potentially fit into the picture. Of course, after you know what tools people are using, you can also ask about the effectiveness of those tools and how easy (or difficult) to use they are. Unlocking these insights will allow you to further personalize the conversations you're having and to better evaluate the potential customers you're having those conversations with.

Use Data to Have Better Conversations

By asking the right questions (and paying attention to the answers), you'll be able to learn more about your potential customers than you ever could using lead capture forms. Instead of feeling like they're entering data into a spreadsheet, with conversational marketing and sales potential customers feel like they're actually being listened to (and that's because they are). As I've already mentioned, the old marketing and sales playbook emphasized being data-driven over being customer-driven. However, that's not to say that you shouldn't use data to make better decisions . . . or to have better conversations.

While using messaging on your website, lots of useful data can be displayed automatically in the conversation window. For example, if you're talking to anonymous visitors—people you don't have email addresses for yet—you'll still be able to see what page of your website they're on, their IP address, their location (city and country), their local time, the operating system and web browser they're using, as well as the number of conversations they've had with you (see Figure 8.1). This is all basic data that a conversational marketing and sales platform can surface automatically for every new conversation you have.

This data can help you have better, more personalized conversations, as you're not going into those conversations completely cold. Even when you're talking to anonymous visitors, you have some insight into who those people are, and you can use that your advantage. For example, if you see that the person you're talking to is in Boston, Massachusetts, you could ask, "What's the weather like in Boston today?" as an icebreaker. Or, if you see that the person you're

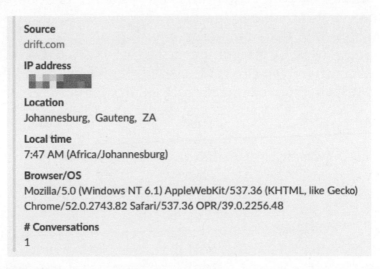

FIGURE 8.1 The profile of an anonymous visitor on the Drift.com homepage.

talking to is currently on your pricing page, you could say something like, "Hey, noticed you were on our pricing page. Any pricing questions I can help you with?"

But to reiterate, this is just basic data you can use to have better conversations. We've really just scraped the surface of the types of insights you can unlock. Specifically, with the rise of data enrichment technology, marketing and sales teams can now access tons of demographic and firmographic data about the people they're talking to and use that data to further personalize the buying experience.

Data Enrichment

Data enrichment refers to the process of taking raw data and enhancing it, refining it, or otherwise improving upon it to make it more valuable. As a marketer or salesperson, after you've captured a person's email address during a conversation, you can use a data enrichment solution to automatically scrape the web for relevant public data associated with that email address. This "enriched" data you collect can include a person's name, LinkedIn URL, LinkedIn profile photo, employment information, and more (see Figure 8.2).

In the past, tracking down this data for all of your leads would require conducting hundreds if not thousands of searches and then manually entering everything into a database. Now, by integrating messaging with a data enrichment solution, you can get this important background data instantly (without having to do a bunch of tedious, repetitive

FIGURE 8.2 Here's what data enrichment can tell us about Drift's head of marketing, Dave Gerhardt, based on his email address.

work) and gain a deeper understanding of the potential customers you're talking to.

IP Address Matching

Of course, there are some potential customers who will come to your website over and over, ask questions, but never leave an email address. Until recently, it was impossible to figure out who these people were, or whether or not they might be a good fit to buy. But here's the thing: With data enrichment technology, an email address isn't the only marker you can use to identify people. You can also use their IP addresses.

With IP address matching, a data enrichment solution looks at the IP address of the person you're talking to and matches it to the domain name of the company that person works at. From there, there are dozens more data points that can be surfaced, including the name of the company, the number of employees who work there, their industry, where they're located, the amount of funding they've raised, as well as links to their LinkedIn and Twitter profiles (see Figure 8.3). Needless to say, for B2B companies, this technology has made life much, much easier, and has freed up marketers and salespeople so they can focus on more important tasks.

Thanks to IP address matching, you can now identify leads who might have otherwise gone unnoticed. What's more, as a B2B company, you can now monitor to see

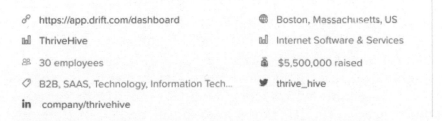

FIGURE 8.3 An example of the results IP matching can return for an anonymous visitor.

whether multiple people from the same company are dropping by your website—a sure sign that that company is interested in buying.

However, it's important to remember that, while the information you learn about potential customers through data enrichment and IP address matching can be helpful, it's no replacement for what you can learn by having actual conversations.

Score the Leads You Talk to (and Send the Best Ones to Sales)

While data can help us uncover objective facts about the people we're talking to, the lead qualification process is, overall, highly subjective. After having conversations with the same person, one marketer or sales rep might decide that he or she is a great fit, while another marketer or sales rep might reach the opposite conclusion.

In order to solve the consistency problem, you need to come up with a set of shared guidelines. Instead of thinking of lead qualification as a binary system, where leads are either qualified or not qualified, you need to think about lead qualification as a spectrum. At the low end are people you shouldn't put in touch with Sales, and at the high end are people you should be opening up a "fast lane" for and putting in touch with Sales immediately.

The Conversation-Qualified Lead Spectrum

As we explored in Chapter Four, once you adopt conversational marketing and sales, you'll be able to switch your focus from marketing-qualified leads (MQLs) and sales-qualified leads (SQLs) to Conversation-Qualified Leads (CQLs)—people who express intent to buy during one-to-one conversations. However, as we discovered at Drift, there are varying degrees to which people can show intent. So to keep all of our marketers and salespeople on the same page, we came up with the following guidelines. They explain what the different levels of being a CQL look like, although they start by explaining what an unqualified lead looks like. Let's dive in.

- **Not qualified.** This is someone who might not understand exactly what your product does and needs to do more research on his or her own to see what your company is all about. People who fall into this category definitely should not be put in contact with a member of your sales team. (However, this doesn't mean that they won't become CQLs at some point.)
- **Good lead.** Someone who has come to your website, is asking about your product or service, and is eager to learn more. Make sure your sales team or BDR team talks to these leads while they are on your website so you can answer their questions and help them move through your sales funnel.
- **Better lead.** This is a good lead who's taken the next step of visiting your pricing page and/or is now asking questions about specific features and pricing plans. Instead of routing these types of leads to a BDR team for further qualification, you could ask whether they'd be interested in booking a product demo with your sales team. If the answer is "Yes," you can drop a sales rep's calendar directly into a conversation with just a few clicks and let people pick the dates and times that works best for them.
- **Best lead.** This is someone who shows up on your website and is immediately interested in scheduling a demo and/or connecting with a sales rep in order to discuss using your product or service for his or her company's specific use case. These are the leads you want to get on Sales' radar as soon as possible.

Applying CQL Scores

At Drift, we've baked this CQL spectrum into our conversational marketing and sales platform, which allows us to score CQLs during conversations by simply clicking one of four buttons (see Figure 8.4). These buttons, which correspond to the different types of CQLs along the CQL spectrum, use lightning bolt icons to represent quality. The more bolts, the better the CQL. And after you apply a CQL

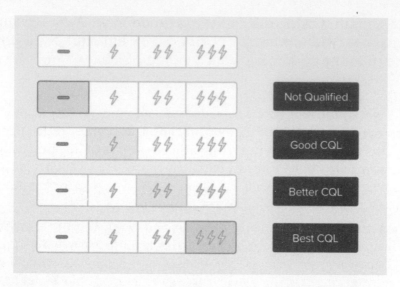

FIGURE 8.4 A breakdown of how we score CQLs at Drift using lightning bolts.

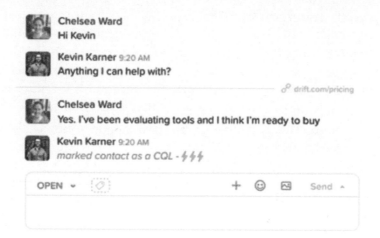

FIGURE 8.5 An example of what manually scoring a CQL looks like.

score, that score (and the accompanying bolts) will show up in a lead's profile anytime you or anyone at your company have a conversation with that lead.

As a marketer or salesperson, you can manually score CQLs using this type of system while having one-to-one, human-to-human conversations (see Figure 8.5). You can also set up routing rules so that as soon as you mark a conversation with three bolts, a sales rep automatically gets added to the conversation.

Qualifying Leads at Scale

Of course, when you're using one-to-one conversations to qualify leads, scalability is an obvious concern. Ultimately, you can take two steps in order to deliver a conversational lead qualification experience at scale. One step, as we'll explore in Chapter Ten, is to set up chatbots that can automate the lead qualification process, and the other step, as we'll explore next, in Chapter Nine, is to filter out the "noise" and focus on having conversations only with your best leads.

Chapter 9

Step Four: Filter Out the Noise and Target Your Best Leads

The most common objection I hear from companies when it comes to having real-time conversations with their website visitors is: "Our marketers and salespeople will end up wasting their time talking to a bunch of random people who are never going to buy." And when you look back at the history of using messaging (also known as "live chat") on your website, it's easy to see why these opinions persist.

Using earlier iterations of messaging technology, companies were able to engage with website visitors in real time, but there was no way for them to fine-tune the flow of conversations. Once the conversation floodgates opened, they remained open, and for companies with high volumes of website traffic, the marketers and sales reps responsible for managing all of those conversations soon became overwhelmed. While some of the people starting those conversations were undoubtedly leads, identifying them among the sea of existing customers, free users, and random visitors, all of whom were chiming in via messaging, could feel like searching for a needle in a haystack. There was simply too much "noise" drowning out the signal.

Today, you no longer need to use messaging as a one-size-fits-all lead generation channel on your website. And you're no longer obligated to offer it as a communication channel to every single person who drops by. Instead, after you get messaging up and running, you can evaluate how many conversations you're having each day, week, and month, and then make adjustments accordingly. If your conversation volume is low, you may find that keeping messaging available to everyone who's visiting your website makes sense. However, if you're seeing lots of conversations come in, and the process is starting to become unmanageable, that's a sign that you need to fine-tune your targeting. Here's how you do it.

Where to Start: Targeting the High-Intent Pages on Your Site

One of the benefits of using messaging is that you're able to create a fast lane for your best leads and engage with them in real time, while they're live on your website and clearly interested in learning more. In many cases, those leads are hanging out on a few specific pages, perhaps on your pricing page or on a bottom-of-the-funnel landing page where they can fill out a form in order to connect with your sales team. These are both examples of high-intent pages—pages on your website that people tend to visit when they're getting close to making a purchase decision. By creating custom welcome messages that target your high-intent pages, you can cut through the "noise" that you might commonly encounter on your homepage or on your blog and hone in on just those visitors who are more likely to buy.

At Drift, our pricing page was one of the first pages we targeted after adding messaging to our website. And while at first we had our custom welcome message appear to everyone who visited the page, we soon refined it in order to make it more selective. Instead of targeting visitors based solely on where they currently are on our website, we now also factor in their recent behavior as part of our "display when" conditions (as in, the welcome message *displays when* these conditions are met).

Targeting Visitors Based on Their On-Site Behavior

In some cases, targeting specific pages on your website might not do a sufficient job of filtering out unqualified visitors. So in order to fine-tune your messaging strategy even further, you can target visitors based on specific behaviors they display while visiting those pages and/or based on behaviors they've displayed in the past.

For example, at Drift, our marketing team has set up the custom welcome message on our pricing page (see Figure 9.1) so that it only displays when the following conditions are met:

- A visitor stays on our pricing page for longer than 45 seconds
- That visitor has visited more than five pages of our website
- That visitor has visited our pricing page specifically at least three times

Because we know that the people who see this welcome message have been on our website before, we're able to call that out in the copy. Instead of saying "Welcome," we can say, "Welcome back," which is exactly what a repeat customer might hear in a brick-and-mortar store. And, of course, because we know what page of our website people

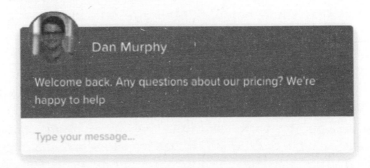

FIGURE 9.1 The custom welcome message we display on our pricing page (for visitors who match our target criteria).

are on when they see this message, we can reference that page specifically in our message as well.

In addition to targeting visitors based on how many pages they've visited, which pages they've visited, and how long they stay on a page, there are several other behaviors you can factor in. For example, you can target visitors based on the number of days since their last visit to your website and/or based on how far they scroll down after landing on a particular page. With the latter, you can set a scroll percentage, such as 25%, or 50%, so that your welcome message only appears to people who have taken the time to explore more of the page. Another behavior you can factor into your targeting equation is exit intent. Exit intent is when a visitor goes to change browser tabs (or to close a tab or window) and the cursor leaves the window up at the top half of the screen. By having a message appear on exit intent, you can grab the attention of visitors right before they leave and, ideally, convince them to stick around.

Targeting Visitors Based On the Sites They're Coming From

Just as the pages visitors are looking at on your website can tell you something about their intent, so can the pages those visitors are coming from—and I don't just mean on your own site. By targeting visitors based on their referrers, whether that's Google or Facebook or an online publication or news site, you'll be able to hone in on specific types of visitors and create incredibly tailored experiences.

An early adopter of this type of targeted messaging was Jake Peters, CEO of the knowledge base software company HelpDocs. Like many tech entrepreneurs, Jake is an active user of the product discovery website Product Hunt, so when he launched Help-Docs in 2016, he coordinated to have a friend "hunt" his new product—which is Product Hunt–speak for having someone share your new product with the community. Once HelpDocs was up on Product Hunt, Jake, along with his co-founder Jarratt Isted, snapped into action and began responding to comments and encouraging people to upvote. The more upvotes, the more people see your product, and, ultimately, the more referral traffic you get back to your company's website.

HelpDocs finished its first day on Product Hunt with more than 200 upvotes and 1,800 new visitors checking out the Help-Docs website. For a startup, that's a lot of eyeballs, and Jake and Jarratt wanted to capitalize on all the website traffic they were generating. In the past, they would have simply relied on lead capture forms and then they would have followed up with everyone later. After all, it was just the two of them. But as Jake told the Drift marketing team, "People want to interact with other people. It should be obvious, right? But traditional contact forms and old-school messaging apps have made it hard. Forms add friction to people getting in touch. If people have a question, they expect an answer right away today. And if you can't deliver and respond to leads quickly, they might disappear forever. We didn't want to miss out on sales from Product Hunt because people had unanswered questions."

Jake's solution: He set up a customized welcome message, featuring his own smiling face (see Figure 9.2), which appeared only for visitors coming from Product Hunt. The message promoted "something special" for those visitors, and when they clicked on the messaging icon, a discount code appeared that they could use to receive 50% off of their Help-Docs subscription for the first six months (see Figure 9.3).

Of course, because this offer was being powered by messaging (and not a lead capture form), many Product Hunters took the opportunity to ask questions while they were on the HelpDocs website. Given that it was launch day, and they had a bunch of other tasks to manage, Jake and Jarratt knew there was no way they'd be able to respond to every potential customer in real time (as much as they wanted to). So they set up a chatbot to act as their backup.

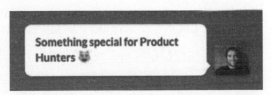

FIGURE 9.2 The custom welcome message HelpDocs created for visitors coming from the Product Hunt website.

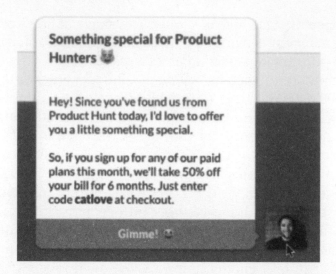

FIGURE 9.3 The big reveal: What targeted visitors saw after clicking HelpDocs' customized welcome message.

As Jake explained to the Drift marketing team, the chatbot "helped out a ton by managing and triaging our inbound leads." Instead of leaving people waiting without a response, the chatbot "kept them in the loop with what was happening. He asked if people were looking to talk to sales or support, then routed the conversations to the right person on our team." The chatbot routed sales conversations to Jarrett and support conversations to Jake, but could also hop in and answer questions as needed (thanks to a knowledge base integration). As Jake explained, "The bot did a great job of keeping our paying customers happy while we were dealing with a higher-than-usual volume of conversations from Product Hunt."

Targeting Visitors Based On the Companies They Work For

As we explored in Chapter Eight, integrating messaging with an enriched data solution allows you to reveal troves of useful data, not only about the people you have email addresses for but also for anonymous visitors. Specifically, thanks to IP address matching, you can instantly identify the company an anonymous visitor works at and then surface relevant attributes about that company, such as number of employees, the amount of funding they've raised, the technologies they're using on their websites, and their Alexa rank, which is based on how much traffic their websites are receiving. These sets of attributes are known as "firmographics," and for B2B companies, using firmographics can be crucial when it comes to targeting the best leads on your website.

With the same data enrichment integration you use to passively learn about the companies visitors work at when those visitors start conversations with you, you can also actively target visitors who work at companies that match your target criteria. This is something former Perfecto Mobile CMO Chris Willis did on the Perfecto Mobile website. As I mentioned in Chapter Six, Chris set up messaging as a "second net" for engaging with and capturing leads who weren't filling out Perfecto Mobile's lead capture forms. But in order to ensure that his sales development reps (SDRs), who were responsible for managing incoming conversations, didn't get bogged down by random visitors who were never going to buy, Chris used IP address matching to hone in on companies that fell within a particular size range.

As Chris told the Drift marketing team, "Our leads tend to be 70% out of our target, 30% in. Now, I expected with web chat we'd see about the same thing. So people chatting and just essentially taking up the time of our SDRs when they could be working on more productive activities." However, after setting up targeted welcome messages, Chris discovered right away that he could easily filter out the "noise" he had been worried about. To quote Chris: "And so right out of the gate, we identified that we were going to see the ability to manage that process. So we're able to, by IP address, identify companies by their size, and only present to our SDRs chats that come from companies that we want to sell to."

At Drift, we use a similar approach in order to set up a fast lane for our best leads. Specifically, we display a custom welcome message (see Figure 9.4) to B2B, SaaS companies that have more than 50 employees. As we looked back on our conversation data, we found that those were the types of companies that

FIGURE 9.4 An example of a targeted welcome message we use on the Drift website that relies on firmographic data.

were more likely to convert into customers, so it made sense to set up a customized path to purchase just for them. And remember, since the firmographic data we're using to target visitors is sourced via a person's IP address, that means even anonymous visitors—people who had never been to your website before—can receive your personalized welcome messages.

Now, if you wanted to take the personalization a step further, you could include the name of the company an anonymous visitor works at in your welcome message (see Figure 9.5). Thanks to IP address matching, it's possible. In fact, not only is it possible, but it can help you grab people's attention and engage more leads in conversation.

One of the pioneers of this type of targeting was Guillaume Cabane, current vice president of growth at Drift and the former

FIGURE 9.5 A mockup of how you can personalize a welcome message based on company name.

vice president of growth at the marketing data SaaS company Segment. During his time at Segment, Guillaume recognized that he was missing out on potential customers by not providing a real-time communication channel using messaging. However, he also knew that only around 10% of the people who visited the Segment website were an ideal fit for his company's product. Guillaume needed a way to filter out the 90% of people who weren't a good fit to talk to their sales team. And when it came to their free users, this is what Guillaume told the Drift marketing team: "16% of our signups represent 86% of our revenue. Those are the people we want to talk to."

In order to be able to target those exact types of buyers, Guillaume integrated messaging with a lead-scoring tool and, after analyzing the firmographic data of companies that had already bought from Segment, he built a predictive lead-scoring model. He then used that model to score anonymous visitors (based on the companies they worked at) as soon as they landed on the Segment website. Visitors from companies that scored high enough were shown personalized welcome messages that called out companies by name. Case in point: When I went to the Segment website, I would see a welcome message that said, "We have advice for Drift." And when you clicked on that message, it would trigger a call-to-action (CTA) to connect with a sales rep (see Figure 9.6).

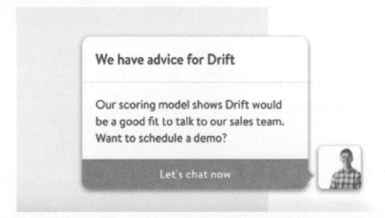

FIGURE 9.6 One of Segment's targeted welcome messages, personalized for Drift.

Within the first three weeks of implementing this targeted, personalized approach, messaging became the third-highest source of the company's qualified leads. Within a few months, it was their number one source. Overall, Guillaume was able to double the number of opportunities they were generating for Sales each month via messaging. Not only were Segment's customers happy with the new streamlined, personalized buying experience, but Segment's sales reps were happy as well. Finally, they were able to separate the signal from the noise and tap into a steady flow of qualified leads.

Feeling Overwhelmed?

For some marketing and sales reps, words like "firmographics" and "predictive lead scoring" might lead you to believe that all of this stuff is really complicated and that only growth experts and mad scientists (like Guillaume) can pull it off. In reality, with a conversational marketing and sales platform, you can easily integrate data enrichment tools and lead scoring tools in order to create a system that can evaluate and target leads automatically. While such integrations are no replacement for using actual conversations in order to qualify leads, they can help ensure you're starting conversations with the right people and that your sales reps are making the best use of their time.

Other Targeting Options for Increasing Conversion Rates

There are dozens upon dozens of other "display when" conditions you can choose from—and countless ways you can combine them—in order to pinpoint the best leads on your company's website. Here are some of the most common types of targeting we haven't covered yet (and how you can use them to improve website conversions).

Targeting by Location

For companies that only sell their products or services in specific geographic regions, this one's a no-brainer. Whether it's a specific country (or specific countries), or if you're based in the United States, a specific state (or specific states), you can fine-tune your messaging to display only when people in those locations visit your site. By targeting just those visitors who live in the locations you cover, you'll be able to significantly improve your company's signal-to-noise ratio.

Targeting by Device

Conversational marketing and sales isn't just about talking to potential customers, it's about talking to them on *their* terms, meeting them where they are, and having relevant conversations. If you're a company that just launched a new mobile app and you're using messaging to drive new sign-ups, showing the same, one-size-fits-all welcome message to all of your visitors isn't the best option. Think about it: Some of your visitors are using desktops or laptops to visit your site, which means if you share a download link for your new mobile app with them, that's not very useful. So instead, why not wait to target those visitors when they're using smartphones or tablets to visit your site? By creating a custom welcome message that targets visitors by device type, you can help make the buying process—or in this case, mobile app signup process—more streamlined.

Targeting Visitors You've Cookied

As many of you already know, a cookie is a tiny bit of data that websites can store in the browsers of their visitors. Remember in Chapter Seven, when I explained how you can display custom welcome messages to website visitors who you've also been communicating with via email? Cookies—and targeting visitors based on those cookies—make that possible. You can also use cookies to hide messaging from certain types of visitors. For example, the hypothetical mobile app company I mentioned in the previous section could use cookies to hide their website's welcome message from visitors who have already downloaded and logged into their app. Also worth noting: For companies that like to A/B test everything, you can use cookies—in combination with an A/B testing service—to target a specific cohort of visitors so you can test different variations of your welcome messages.

Targeting Segments

While messaging has always been beneficial as a reactive channel for businesses, targeting is what allows it to be proactive. And just as with traditional marketing automation tools, you can use targeted messaging to engage with specific lists of contacts—or segments—that your company has already built (or is continuing to build).

For seasoned marketers and salespeople, the terms "static segment" and "dynamic segment" are likely very familiar. But let's do a quick review of how they apply to the world of messaging.

- **Static Segments.** This is a list of contacts that remains unchanged until you manually add people to it (or remove people from it). You'd most likely want to target static segments when sending one-off messaging campaigns. For example, if you wanted to use messaging to promote an event to a select group of leads, you could target a static segment made up of those leads.

- **Dynamic Segments.** A dynamic segment is a list of contacts that is ever-changing. Often used for nurturing, onboarding, and retention, you can customize the rules of who's added to dynamic segments based on a wide variety of criteria. For example, as a SaaS company, if you wanted to build an ongoing messaging campaign designed to re-engage inactive users, you could target a dynamic segment made up of users who were last active in your product more than 30 days ago. You could also use dynamic segments in order to hone in on free users who have visited your pricing page recently (and therefore might be interested in upgrading) and for reaching out to users who aren't satisfied with your product (based on their recent Net Promoter Score or NPS).

You'll learn more about how you can apply the same strategies you use in conversational marketing and sales to customer support and customer success in Part IV of the book.

Right now, it's time for you to learn how to build a chatbot.

Chapter 10

Step Five: Build a Lead Qualification Chatbot (Without Writing a Single Line of Code)

A common criticism I hear when it comes to chatbots is that businesses often treat them as novelties. Instead of identifying actual problems that chatbots would be well-suited to solve, some businesses simply insert chatbots into their online marketing as a way to appear modern and to generate buzz. That's why, at Drift, we started out with a philosophy before we developed any technology. We established from the very beginning that we would only use chatbots where it made sense to use them—for performing tedious, repetitive tasks that sapped up the time of marketers and salespeople. We identified real problems that thousands of marketing and sales teams (ours included) were experiencing on a daily basis and built chatbots that could solve those problems as quickly and efficiently as possible before getting out of the way.

One of the biggest problems we were able to solve with the help of a chatbot was qualifying leads in real time. As we learned back in Chapter Three, the rise of messaging has made it infinitely easier to have conversations with your website visitors, but the number of conversations you're having can sometimes become unmanageable. And when your team is offline, it's possible that some potential customers on your website could end up slipping away. This was something everyone at Drift hated: knowing that potential customers were coming to our website, but not being able to qualify them all in real time. So in 2017, we built and launched LeadBot, an intelligent marketing and sales assistant designed specifically for qualifying leads without relying on lead capture forms (or humans).

In addition to serving as "backup" for marketers and salespeople when they're offline or when they experience a sudden influx of conversations, LeadBot and other lead qualification chatbots give you the ability to precisely control the volume and quality of leads that you're generating on your website. Remember in the previous chapter, when we explored all of the different ways you can target messaging in order to hone in on your best leads? You can use those same targeting conditions with lead qualification chatbots, which means you can set up custom chatbots for particular audiences and have those chatbots ask hyper-relevant qualifying questions.

Instead of forcing human marketers and sales reps to ask the same few qualifying questions over and over and over, chatbots streamline the process. The overall experience ends up being better for buyers, as they're able to learn right away whether or not your product is the right fit for them, and if it is, they can be connected with Sales instantly. There's no need to wait for a follow-up email or phone call. As marketers and salespeople, meanwhile, we have more of our day back to focus on actually marketing and selling and having conversations with the right people. According to research from Marketo, a 5% increase in selling time can lead to a 20% increase in revenue. So just imagine what would happen if your sales reps didn't have to waste time waiting for form submissions and blasting out follow-up emails. By using a lead qualification chatbot, you can put your sales funnel on autopilot and qualify leads 24 hours a day. Best of all, setting up one of these chatbots doesn't require writing a single line of code and only takes a few minutes. Here's how you do it.

Coming Up with Questions and Responses for Your Bot

While it might sound technical, setting up a lead qualification chatbot on your website is really an exercise in crafting conversations. It's about coming up with interesting questions, anticipating the responses you might get, and then writing relevant follow-ups based on those responses. Unlike a lead capture form, a lead qualification chatbot doesn't passively collect answers, but actively engages visitors in one-to-one conversation and learns about those visitors just as a human marketer or sales rep would. But to clarify, the goal here isn't to have the chatbot convince your website visitors that it's human; the goal is to be able to provide a high-quality, real-time buying experience on your website, even when the humans on your team are unavailable.

Chances are, your marketing and/or sales team already have the bones of a lead qualification chatbot built out, either in the form of a lead capture form or in the form of a sales script. So to start, you'll want to identify the two or three "must ask" questions that you've already been asking on your forms and/or during sales conversations and turn those into a script for your bot.

Of course, the specific questions marketing and sales teams have lead qualification chatbots ask will vary from company to company and industry to industry. But as a starting point, I recommend following the "What? Who? How?" template we came up with at Drift (see Table 10.1).

TABLE 10.1	The "What? Who? How?" approach to writing a lead qualification script for a chatbot.	
Chatbot Question 1	*What* brought you here?
Chatbot Question 2	*Who* are you?
Chatbot Question 3	*How* can I help you use our product?

Keep reading to see how we've used this template at Drift and how you can customize it for your own business.

Question 1: What?

If a first-time customer walked into your brick-and-mortar store, one of the first questions you might ask is, "What can I help you with today?" or "What brings you here today?" At first glance, this might seem like a benign question or just a simple greeting, but for marketers and salespeople, it can help surface a website visitor's intent.

At Drift, we had the first iteration of our lead qualification chatbot (named Driftbot) start conversations by asking, "What brought you here to check out Drift?" We then scripted custom follow-ups based on people's answers. For example, if people answered that they heard about us via our Seeking Wisdom podcast, we'd have the chatbot encourage them to leave the podcast a five-star review and subscribe before it moved onto the next question (see Figure 10.1).

Question 2: Who?

This next question can be asked in a variety of ways, most of which don't necessarily require the use of the word "who." At Drift, we've often expressed this question through asking, "What website are you looking to use Drift on?" A common alternative: "What company do you represent?"

For B2B companies, this bit of information is crucial. It can help you prioritize conversations and figure out which of your human sales reps will ultimately be assigned to particular leads—assuming those leads end up being qualified.

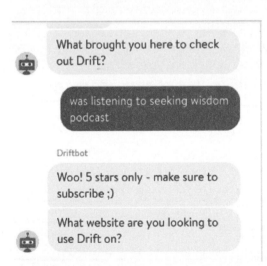

FIGURE 10.1 The first two questions from our original lead qualification chatbot script at Drift.

While you can sometimes reveal this information via a data enrichment tool, as we explored in Chapter Eight, the success rates of those tools aren't always 100%. In some cases, anonymous visitors will remain anonymous...unless you engage them in conversation and ask them who they are.

Question 3: How?

Once a chatbot has identified *what* a person is doing on your website, as well as *who* that person is, it'll be time to dig deeper and have the chatbot figure out *how* you can help that person use your product.

At Drift, we've often used the variation, "How are you looking to use Drift?" and have then listed "sales," "marketing," and "support" as potential options (see Figure 10.2). Regardless of the copy you use, the goal here is to gather enough context so that if a lead ends up being qualified, the sales rep on your team that joins the conversation and takes the sale over the finish line won't be going into that conversation cold. Instead, the sales rep who ends up talking to a chatbot-qualified lead will already have at least a basic understanding of who that qualified lead is and how he or she can help—thanks to the information gathered by chatbots.

Whether you're using lead forms or chatbots, asking the right questions is crucial to any lead qualification strategy. And while we recommend starting small and only having your chatbot ask two or three questions in the beginning, there's no reason that you can't eventually transfer every question you have on your lead capture forms over to

FIGURE 10.2 The third question from our original lead qualification chatbot script at Drift.

a lead qualification chatbot (or to a small fleet of chatbots that target different audiences).

But remember: What sets chatbots apart is that they're able to elicit information conversationally. In addition to asking questions, they can respond to what website visitors tell them, and that's what makes the experience so engaging.

For marketers and salespeople, copying and pasting the questions you've already been asking is phase one of building a lead qualification chatbot. Phase two is coming up with the perfect responses—the follow-ups that chatbots give after leads answer your qualifying questions. These follow-up responses are what really bring your chatbot conversations to life and help prevent them from feeling like carbon copies of your forms. They offer you a chance to show off your brand's personality.

Setting Up Responses

There are two different ways you can approach writing chatbot responses: by basing them on keywords that visitors use when answering open-ended questions, or by basing them on button responses—which you've pre-written—that visitors click on.

In both cases, there's a bit of setup work involved, which is why I recommend starting small and only asking a few questions when setting up your first lead qualification chatbot. Once you understand how both options work, you can go back and fine-tune your chatbot, updating your questions and building out more responses as needed.

1. Using keywords. By crafting responses that align to certain keywords or sets of keywords, your lead qualification chatbot can ask your website visitors open-ended questions and—provided there's a keyword match—reply with customized responses.

Earlier in the chapter (see Figure 10.1), you saw an example of keyword matching in action. At Drift, after asking "What brought you here to check out Drift?" our chatbot would analyze the responses of website visitors and

FIGURE 10.3 Example of a list of keywords we used at Drift that would trigger a custom chatbot response about our podcast.

try to match them to the keyword list we had built behind the scenes (see Figure 10.3), inside of our conversational marketing and sales platform. We would link each keyword to a pre-written response, so that—for example—visitors who mentioned the name of our podcast, Seeking Wisdom, or even the word "podcast," would receive that customized message which, as I mentioned before, encouraged them to leave a five-star review and to subscribe.

This type of customization is possible thanks to some simple keyword matching. All it takes is listing some keywords and writing some corresponding responses. The tricky part is making sure you have all of your bases covered and that you have pre-loaded responses primed and ready for every eventuality.

At Drift, we realized early on that keyword matching can be inefficient. With so many potential ways people could reply to our questions, it was hard to craft the perfect responses to match every scenario. So, as you saw in Figure 10.2, even in the earliest iteration of our lead qualification chatbot, we suggested answers in order to help steer

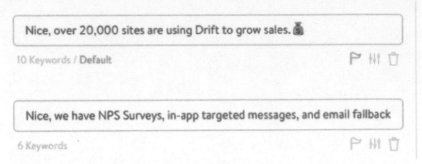

FIGURE 10.4 Setting up chatbot responses (top response = people who mention sales, bottom response = people who mention support).

conversations in the right directions. Instead of just asking, "How are you looking to use Drift?" we included a small addendum in parentheses and gave people some options: "(sales, marketing, support, etc.)."

Behind the scenes, we set up keyword lists based around the keywords "sales," "marketing," and "support," and then crafted custom responses for each keyword. For people who mentioned sales, for example, the chatbot would respond by saying, "Nice, over 20,000 sites are using Drift to grow sales." (We also stuck a money bag emoji at the end for good measure.) For people who mentioned support, meanwhile, we had the chatbot respond by talking about the support-related features of our product, such as in-app messaging (see Figure 10.4).

And while guiding people with your questions can increase the likelihood of your chatbot providing a relevant response, there's no way you can come up with a custom response for every single thing a person might say. That's why when setting up chatbot responses using keywords, it's important that you also choose a default response—a pre-selected response that will appear when your chatbot can't match any of your keywords. By establishing a default response, you can ensure the chatbot keeps the conversation going (even if it's not 100% sure what someone was trying to say).

A default response could be something as simple as "Hmmm. OK." Or you could use it to highlight a specific feature or selling point of your product, which, as was the case with suggesting answers in your questions, can help you steer the conversation in the right direction. At Drift, we originally had our chatbot use the same response we showed to people who were interested in using Drift for sales (see Figure 10.4) as our default response to our third qualifying question, as it highlighted some social proof related to our customers. That way, even if the chatbot couldn't find a keyword match, it could still keep the conversation going and help people learn more about our product.

2. Using button responses. While keyword matching is perhaps the more natural way of getting your lead qualification chatbot to provide relevant responses, as your visitors are able to use natural language when answering qualifying questions, button responses allow for a speedier qualification process. Instead of having your chatbot ask open-ended questions, with button responses, you can make your questions multiple choice.

For example, instead of having your chatbot start a conversation by asking the open-ended question, "What brought you to our site?" then hoping the answer someone gives matches one of your keywords, you can have your chatbot ask that question while simultaneously displaying buttons with pre-written answers such as "Want to talk to sales" or "just browsing" (see Figure 10.5). As was the case with using keywords, you can create customized responses that are linked to those answers.

Ultimately, keyword matching and button responses both have their

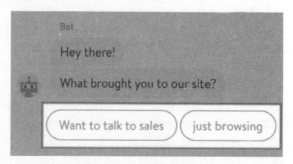

FIGURE 10.5 A mockup of how you can use button responses when setting up your lead qualification chatbot.

advantages. Button responses are especially useful in the early stages of a conversation, as they can help you quickly and easily organize your website visitors into two piles: people who are ready to buy and interested in talking to sales and people who are still just learning and looking around. Meanwhile, once a lead has moved further down your funnel, having your chatbot ask open-ended questions can help you reveal more granular details about potential customers, such as the specific business metrics they're trying to improve and by how much they're trying to move those metrics. Human sales reps can then review these answers and use the insights they uncover to enter sales conversations with tons of context.

Tying Responses to Actions

When crafting your chatbot's responses, you'll also need to choose corresponding actions to accompany those responses. Otherwise, your chatbot won't know how to proceed. For example, if someone gives a qualifying answer to your first question, your chatbot should—after acknowledging that answer with a response—promptly move onto the second question and keep the conversation going. Alternatively, if a person gives an invalid answer to that question, your chatbot could ask the same question again.

Now, if someone gives a disqualifying answer to your first question, indicating that he or she is not a good fit to buy, you may choose to end the conversation right then and there. When ending conversations, you can have your chatbot deliver a customized sign-off message that lets the person know why he or she isn't a good fit. Or you could keep it even simpler and write something like, "Sorry, we don't think our product is a good fit for you at the moment."

Behind the scenes, controlling who proceeds to your chatbot's next question and who doesn't requires ticking a few boxes. For each response you've written for your chatbot, you simply need to choose a corresponding action. When chatting with qualified leads, this action will typically be moving on to the next question—that is, until you reach your final question.

Deciding On a Call-to-Action (CTA)

Whether you use keyword matching, button responses, or a combination of both, once you've set up your questions and the corresponding responses, you will have the makings of a chatbot that can work toward a specific goal. As a lead qualification chatbot, that goal is to identify people who are likely to buy by engaging them in conversation and persuading them to answer a few questions.

Now, let's imagine that a website visitor has replied to all of the chatbot's questions and, based on the answers that he or she has given, it's clear that this person is a great fit to buy. In other words, let's imagine that a chatbot has succeeded in its goal. It begs the obvious question: What should that chatbot do next?

At Drift, when a chatbot successfully qualifies a lead and a conversation reaches its natural conclusion, we have the chatbot automatically apply a conversation-qualified lead (CQL) score—something we learned about back in Chapter Four. We also have the chatbot tag the conversation as being "bot-qualified," which allows us to distinguish between CQLs who were qualified via human-to-human versus chatbot-to-human conversations. (Meanwhile, the leads our chatbot disqualifies during conversations are marked as "disqualified.")

Of course, this all happens behind the scenes. The real action happens on your website, inside of the conversation window. That's because after reaching its goal, the chatbot can automatically display a call-to-action (CTA)—a prompt that encourages qualified leads to talk to a human sales rep, or to book a time on a sales reps' calendar (see Figure 10.6), or to start a free trial of your product, or to simply leave an email address. Ultimately, the CTA you use at the end of your chatbot conversation will depend on what you're trying to accomplish.

Also worth noting: You don't *have* to use CTAs only at the end of your conversations. Hypothetically, if during your first or second qualifying question a person gives an amazing

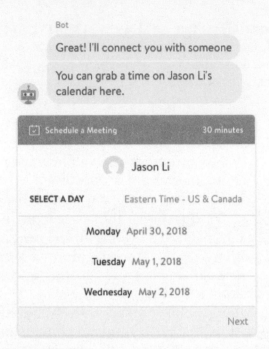

FIGURE 10.6 A mockup of how a chatbot can insert a sale rep's calendar directly into a conversation.

qualifying answer (or indicates that he or she is from an amazing company), you could have the chatbot "fast track" that person and either connect him or her instantly with a sales rep or give immediate access to a sales rep's calendar.

Five Tips for Making Your Chatbot Conversations More Engaging

So far in this chapter I've focused primarily on the mechanics of setting up a lead qualification chatbot. We've seen how your pre-written questions and responses and the follow-up actions you choose establish the flow of the conversational buying process. However, what we haven't spent much time on—yet—is how to make chatbot conversations as enjoyable and as worthwhile for your visitors and potential customers. Here are five tips you should follow:

1. **Keep questions short and sweet**. When you ask broad, complicated questions, you're likely to get broad, complicated answers that don't align with your chatbot's responses. By keeping questions short and sweet, you'll be able to keep people focused and engaged and move them more quickly through your qualification process.

2. **Provide answer options**. As I mentioned earlier, in some instances, having your chatbot ask open-ended questions can make sense. But as a general rule, if you want your chatbot to qualify leads as quickly and as efficiently as possible, providing answer options—especially in the form of button responses— is the way to do it. With button responses, you're likely to get higher levels of engagement, as visitors won't have to rack their brains to come up with original answers.

3. **Be transparent about the fact you're using a chatbot**. For starters, that means you shouldn't use the face of a human employee as the chatbot's avatar. Pet photos, cartoons, and illustrated robots are all good alternatives, as they all help establish that the chatbot on your website is not an actual person. From a copywriting perspective, own the fact that you're using a chatbot and don't be afraid to call it out. For example, you could have a chatbot open a conversation by saying something like, "I know I'm just a chatbot (beep bop boop), but I wanted to see whether I could help." It's better to be upfront about the experience you're providing and to set expectations right away rather than risk tricking people—even if it's accidental.

4. **Come up with paths for every type of visitor**. As marketers and salespeople, we always want to roll out the red carpet for our best leads. But in some cases, that means we end up ignoring website visitors who don't end up being qualified and those people come away with a poor experience. By creating responses and follow-up actions that address those website visitors, you can help set them on the path to becoming qualified later. (At the very least, you can leave them with a positive impression of your brand.) For example, if someone came to your website to read a blog post, he or she probably isn't ready for a sales demo. But that doesn't mean that person wouldn't be interested in signing up for your newsletter. So instead of thinking of a lead qualification chatbot as having a single goal (connecting qualified leads with Sales) and providing a single track for buyers, think about it as having multiple goals and providing

multiple tracks that can cater to all of the different types of people on your website.

5. **Test it out**. Putting a lead qualification chatbot on your website can result in more conversations than your team might be used to managing. That's why before you roll a lead qualification chatbot out to your entire website, or to wherever you're going to display it, you should test it out on a smaller audience. For example, you could target a page on your website, or you could target a segment of people who have visited a certain page of your site a certain number of times, and then observe how the conversations unfold. Are people answering every question or are they getting hung up somewhere? Are multiple people giving an answer you hadn't thought of ahead of time? After a few conversations, you'll be able to identify any gaps in your chatbot script and make adjustments accordingly.

Part III

Converting Conversational Marketing Leads into Sales

Chapter 11

How to Put Your Sales Funnel on Autopilot

Thanks to the rise of messaging and chatbots, which allow us to capture and qualify leads in real time, sales teams are now able to put their sales funnels on autopilot. That means as a sales rep, instead of having to sort through lists of leads and play phone tag (and email tag) with people who have filled out lead capture forms, you can now sit back and wait for sales meetings to appear on your calendar automatically. Whether you're at the beach or stuck in a meeting, a lead qualification chatbot (which we learned how to build in Chapter Ten) can step in and qualify leads for you 24 hours a day, seven days a week.

However, while a lead qualification chatbot makes it possible to scale and automate the lead qualification process—and, more generally, can make everyone's life easier—a chatbot is still no replacement for an actual, human sales rep. So even when autopilot is turned on, sales reps need to pay attention and, when they're online, be ready to engage with leads at a moment's notice.

Throughout this chapter, I'm going to explore some of the tools and tactics sales teams can use in order to drive the best results possible and to ensure leads move through their sales funnels as quickly and as efficiently as possible.

We're going to start by looking at one of the most crucial aspects of any conversational selling strategy: figuring out how new conversations should be routed and, more specifically, which sales reps they should be routed to.

Set Up Routing Rules So Leads Always Are Connected to the Right Sales Reps

For companies with large sales teams, the prospect of opening up a new real-time channel with messaging (and automating it with chatbots) might seem like a logistical nightmare. With so many new leads coming in, how do you fairly and evenly distribute them among your sales reps based on territory and/or company size, or whatever other lead routing rules you are following? The good news: With a conversational marketing and sales platform, you can integrate with your existing CRM, such as Salesforce, and follow the same routing rules you've always been following. That way, when a lead requests to start a conversation (or schedule a demo) with Sales, you can make sure that the sales rep who owns that lead in your CRM is the one who'll be added to the conversation (see Figure 11.1).

For sales teams that don't have existing routing rules already set up in a CRM, you can create new routing rules directly inside a conversational marketing and sales platform, where you'll be able to route leads to specific reps based on a lead's location, website behavior (like number of website visits), firmographics, and other attributes. For example, if you had a sales rep who focused exclusively on

 Danielle Tocci 3:44 PM
joined conversation from routing rule Salesforce Rule

FIGURE 11.1 Mockup of a sales rep being added to a conversation (based on a Salesforce routing rule).

selling to European customers, you could set up your routing rules so only people in European countries who started conversations would be routed to that particular rep.

The Round Robin

For large sales teams, there are often multiple sales reps assigned to each sales territory. So in order to make sure the leads being captured (and qualified) via conversational marketing are being distributed fairly among sales reps, you can set up a "round robin" distribution system. The way it works: First, inside your conversational marketing and sales platform, you select a group (or team) of sales reps that own a specific territory. Then you apply your routing rules to that entire group and distribute new leads to the sales reps in that group on a rotating basis.

If certain sales reps are inactive or offline, you can have the round robin skip over those reps and route leads to reps who are available. In addition to ensuring that leads are distributed evenly and fairly, the round robin system ensures that new leads are connected to available sales reps as soon as possible (which is why our own sales team uses it at Drift).

Use Chatbots to Schedule Sales Meetings 24/7

In Chapter Ten, we explored how marketing and sales teams can build lead qualification chatbots that sit on your website and help move website visitors through your sales funnel at record speeds. As a sales rep, all you have to do is (1) integrate your calendar with your team's conversational marketing and sales platform so leads can book meetings with you and (2) wait for those meetings to appear on your calendar. The chatbot takes care of sending out confirmation emails to both sides and automatically adds the meeting to your calendar. And don't worry: Behind the scenes, you can control which days and times you make available for meetings and demos; that way you're never caught off guard when one appears on your calendar.

Scott Magdalein, the founder of TrainedUp (an online platform for training church volunteers) tweeted the following in May of 2017 after his team started using chatbots to schedule demos: "scheduling bot is going gangbusters. 6 demos a day ain't no joke." TrainedUp's director of marketing, Kevin Fontenot, responded to that tweet with a tweet of his own, which read: "For real though. Jump on a demo and another one magically appears."

By July of 2017, they—and by "they" I mean just the two of them, Scott and Kevin—were using chatbots to book more than 80 qualified demos per month.

Going Outbound

While replacing your lead capture forms with chatbots and having demos "magically" appear on your calendar is certainly an incredible benefit of conversational sales, it's important to remember that, as a sales rep, using conversational sales isn't just about selling to the people who are already on your website—it's about starting conversations with potential customers on their terms, when they're ready to talk. When it comes to outbound sales, you can take advantage of the lead qualification chatbot (or chatbots) your team has already built by using them as outreach tools. You do that by creating custom hyperlinks that trigger chatbot conversations and then sharing those hyperlinks on social media, in emails, in blog posts, or wherever else you want.

If using hyperlinks to trigger conversations sounds familiar, it's because it's exactly the same process I mentioned in Chapter Seven. Only this time, instead of using a hyperlink to trigger a messaging conversation, we're talking about using a hyperlink to trigger a chatbot conversation. By including a link to a chatbot in an outbound email or direct message to a potential customer, you're giving that person the opportunity to self-qualify and to book a meeting with you when it's most convenient for him or her.

Have Your Website's "Contact Sales" CTA Trigger a Real-Time Conversation

In a 2017 report by the Drift marketing team, which analyzed the marketing strategies of the top 100 SaaS companies, we found that 69% of those high-growth companies have CTAs on their websites that prompt people to get in touch with Sales. However, of those 69 companies, only two gave people the opportunity to chat with sales reps in real time after clicking their "Contact" CTAs. The rest directed people either to lead capture forms or to landing pages where people were then instructed to call in or email.

For most sales teams, our "Contact Sales" or "Get a Demo" buttons have been missed opportunities on a massive scale. Think about it: There have been people on our websites raising their hands and saying, "I'm ready to talk to a salesperson," and instead of connecting those people with Sales right away, we've been forcing them to wait. We've been putting them through the same lead form and follow-up system we put every other lead through.

So here's the solution, and it's a simple one: Instead of linking your "Contact Sales" button to a lead capture form, have it link to a real-time conversation instead—either a human-to-human conversation (if you have a sales rep online) or a chatbot-to-human conversation (see Figure 11.2). Either way, as a sales rep, you'll be able to give qualified leads the opportunity to schedule demos with you right away, instead of making them wait for follow-up emails or phone calls. Best of all, you can use the same "round robin" approach to lead routing we talked about earlier to evenly distribute

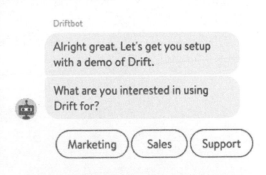

FIGURE 11.2 The chatbot message people see after they click the "Get a Demo" button on the Drift website.

the leads you generate from your website's "Contact Sales" or "Get a Demo" CTA among sales reps.

From a setup perspective, updating your "Contact Sales" CTA relies on the same approach I explained in the previous section. First, you build a chatbot, or set up a messaging campaign, and then you create a hyperlink that will trigger that chatbot or campaign. Once you have the hyperlink, all you need to do is link it to the CTA button on your website and your real-time "Contact Sales" channel will be in place.

Have Sales Reps Create Digital Business Cards

Once you've signed up for a conversational marketing and sales platform and you've connected your calendar—such as through Google or Office 365—you'll be able to build your own "digital business card," which is a public profile with a unique URL that prospects can use to learn more about you as well as to start real-time conversations and book demos with you (see Figure 11.3).

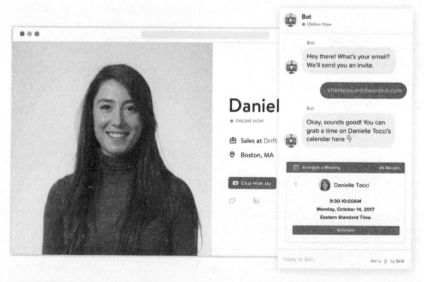

FIGURE 11.3 An example of a Drift salesperson's "digital business card."

At Drift, every employee creates one of these profiles and we use them to share a little bit about ourselves, including our names, locations, roles, as well as some of our interests and hobbies. This helps to further drive home the fact to our potential customers that we (the people they're talking to via real-time messaging) are actual company employees— not anonymous corporate drones. We host these profiles on a subdomain of the Drift website, team.drift.com, and each individual profile has a unique URL. For example, the URL for my profile at Drift is team.drift.com/david.

Unlike when you give someone a traditional business card, when you share a link to your profile with someone— when you give someone a "digital business card"—that person doesn't have to make a phone call or compose an email in order to get in touch with you. Instead, he or she can simply click a button to start a conversation with you in real-time—assuming you're online, of course.

At Drift, we display status indicators on our profiles (little green dots) that let profile visitors know whether or not we're online and available to chat. If we're *not* available to chat at the precise moment a person visits, that person can still leave us a message or he or she can click a second button, which will allow the person to schedule meetings with us directly on our calendars (thanks to the help of a friendly chatbot).

As a sales rep, you can include a link to your digital business card in your email signature, in your social profiles, and you can also drop it into conversations you're having on messaging apps like Messenger and WhatsApp. It's the perfect tool for connecting your existing sales channels to the real-time conversations happening on your website.

Get Real-Time Notifications When Leads Are Online

With most messaging apps, you can opt to receive mobile push notifications on your phone any time someone sends you a message. That way, you can make sure you're able to respond promptly and not miss out on any important conversations. The same holds true with conversational marketing and sales platforms. As a salesperson, you can receive notifications on your phone (as well as through your browser or via email) any time someone starts a conversation on your website. You can also fine-tune your notifications so that, for example, you're only alerted when qualified leads start conversations.

But here's where things get really cool: In addition to receiving notifications after leads start conversations *with you*, you can get notifications as soon as leads land on your website so you can proactively start conversations *with them*. Whether it's a qualified lead you've already chatted with before or a first-time visitor from one of your target accounts, you can set up notifications that will alert you as soon as these types of leads are on your website.

Once you receive one of these notifications, you'll be one click away from proactively starting a real-time conversation with a lead. Or, if it's a mobile push notification, you'll be one swipe away from starting a conversation (see Figure 11.4). Either way, one of the best features of these notifications is that—in addition to letting you know when a lead is on your website—they can tell you exactly what page of your site that lead is on.

As a sales rep, these notifications make it possible for you to proactively start conversations with leads on your website without having to go into those conversations cold. For example, if you were notified that a lead was on your pricing page, you could send that lead a personalized, one-to-one message to let him or her know that you're available to answer any pricing questions that

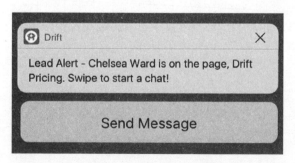

FIGURE 11.4 Mockup of a mobile push notification that's letting you know there's a lead on your pricing page.

FIGURE 11.5 Example of a proactive one-to-one message sent from a sales rep to a lead visiting a company's pricing page.

might arise. To the person visiting your pricing page, this message appears like any other welcome message—the only difference is that it's hyper-personalized (see Figure 11.5).

And while chatbots now make it possible to automate these types of messages, allowing you to provide a conversational experience at scale, that doesn't mean sales team should abandon one-to-one outreach. Sometimes you need to do the things that don't scale in order to provide the best experience possible. Specifically, as a salesperson, when you're online and you can clearly see that there's a lead on your website, why wait for a chatbot to help the person when you could jump in and help him or her yourself? With notifications, you're able to provide the type of personal touch that can help you bring a sale over the finish line.

Behind the scenes, setting up these notifications works a lot like Twitter: In your conversational marketing and sales platform, you simply select the leads (or companies) you want to follow and you'll start receiving notifications when those leads are on your website. Depending on the

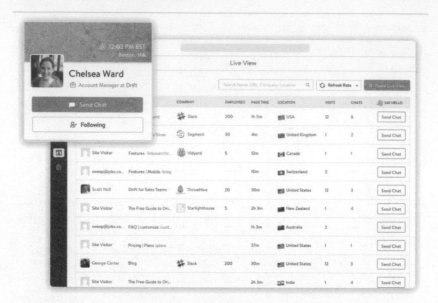

FIGURE 11.6 Mockup of a "live view" screen, which allows you to see (and start conversations with) all of the visitors who are live on your website.

specific platform you're using, you might also be able to see a live view of all of your website visitors. A live view screen (see Figure 11.6) is dynamic, refreshing every time a person visits your website, leaves your website, or navigates to a different page on your website. As a sales rep, you can scan this live view screen and, just as with notifications, start real-time conversations with a single click.

Say Goodbye to Manual Data Entry

According to a 2016 study from CSO Insights, salespeople are currently spending just 36% of their time selling, with the rest of their time going to other activities, such as prospecting, sending out emails, and—you guessed it—data entry. Ask any salesperson what the most tedious and/or annoying aspects of his or her job are, and chances are the answer will include having to update contact records with every phone call, email, meeting, and any other interaction he or she has during the course of a sale. Instead of being able to focus exclusively on providing a great buying experience, sales reps have traditionally had to balance that with manually updating records and making sure they were entering all the data correctly. So it probably won't come as much of a surprise to learn that an earlier study from CSO Insights found that 71% of sales professionals say they spend too much time on data entry.

When you adopt a conversational approach to selling, that manual data entry disappears, allowing sales productivity to skyrocket. That's because when you're having conversations and qualifying leads and booking meetings all in real time, all in one place (your website), you don't need to manually record every little event and detail—a conversational marketing and sales platform can record that for you automatically. (As you'll learn in Chapter Thirteen, it can also keep track of your email conversations).

Through an integration with your existing CRM, you can have all of the information you gather via real-time conversations (for example, names, email addresses, company names, and so on) copied over to your CRM automatically. What's more, you can have transcripts of the conversations you have with leads automatically added to their contact records in your CRM. That way, you'll be able to see everything you've ever learned about a lead and review every conversation you've ever had with that lead in a single, convenient location—no manual data entry required.

What to Do Once Your Sales Funnel Is on Autopilot

Throughout this chapter, I've broken down some of the core ways conversational sales is streamlining the buying process and contributing to better sales productivity. From using an intelligent routing system to make sure leads are connected to the right sales reps, to receiving real-time notifications when a lead visits your website so you can start conversations at the right times, to erasing the need for manual data entry, sales technology has taken some of the most tedious tasks off of Sales' plate. By automating these tedious tasks, sales reps are now able to focus more of their time and energy on the most important part of sales: building relationships through having one-to-one conversations.

In the next chapter, we'll explore how sales teams can harness the power of conversations in order to create a better buying experience and convert more leads into customers.

Chapter 12

How Sales Teams Can Create a Better Buying Experience with Real-Time Conversations

It's time for salespeople to face the facts: The days of the "hard sell" are over. In a world where product information is freely available, and where people have come to expect real-time responses from businesses as the norm, and where owning the demand for a product or service has become more important than owning the supply, it's clear that the traditional sales process has been rendered obsolete.

Today, helping is the new selling.

Think about it: Today, if you lock up white papers and other resources behind lead capture forms, potential buyers can simply go look for that information somewhere else (like on a competitor's website) instead of wasting time filling out your form. Today, if potential buyers try to get in touch with your sales team and you force them to wait weeks, days, or hours before someone actually follows up, it's very likely those potential buyers are going to slip away (and end up turning to a competitor who responds to their inquiries in real time).

Over the past few years, there's been a growing disconnect between the experiences sales teams have traditionally been providing and the experiences modern buyers expect. And this is especially the case in the world of B2B sales.

Today, most B2B sales teams are putting B2B buyers through an experience that bears no resemblance to the buying experiences those buyers are having elsewhere in their lives as consumers. And as former Forrester analyst Andy Hoar once explained on an episode of Forrester's What It Means podcast, people are both aware of—and turned off by—how inferior today's B2B buying experience is when compared to the incredible B2C (business-to-consumer) buying experience they've grown accustomed to. As Hoar explained:

"It's not as though you have a B2C consumer experience that blows you away on Amazon, or Nordstrom, or Sephora, or Charles Schwab, or wherever you're going to go, and then, all of the sudden, go to work and say, 'Well, now I expect a much worse customer experience, and I'm happy with that.'"

The bottom line: Today's B2B buyers expect better, which means as a salesperson, you can no longer rely on the traditional B2B sales playbook. The most successful salespeople of this new sales paradigm—a paradigm where customers have all the power—won't be the salespeople who doggedly pursue and pressure people into buying. Instead, the most successful salespeople will be the ones who guide customers through the buying process, making themselves available to answer questions every step of the way. Instead of "Always be closing," the sales mantra of the future is "Always be helping."

Turning Words into Actions

Of course, while this concept of "helping being the new selling" and providing the best buying experience possible sounds great on paper, it begs the question: As a salesperson, how do you actually do it?

In the previous chapter, we explored the tools and tactics sales teams can use in order to get their conversational sales strategy up and running so they can sell in real time. In this chapter, we'll turn our attention to the specific tactics individual sales reps can use while working on the front lines in order to have better sales conversations.

Ask for Permission Before You Start Asking Questions

The salesperson/buyer relationship can be a tricky one to navigate. Traditionally, as salespeople, we've looked at potential buyers almost as adversaries—as people we've had to "conquer" in order to win over to our side and to our way of thinking. As a result, today there is a lingering tension between salespeople and buyers. Robert Gibbons, VP of sales at the IT management company Ipswitch, refers to this phenomenon as "relationship tension." Robert has trained sales teams all around the world in the art of conversation and he's seen that when it comes to engaging in a one-to-one conversation with a potential buyer, easing this relationship tension as quickly as possible is a crucial first step. Otherwise, it becomes harder for that buyer to trust you and to see you as a resource (and not as an adversary).

How do you ease relationship tension at the beginning of a sales conversation? As Robert told the Drift marketing team, before you launch into your sales script or start going through a list of questions, you need to ask for permission:

"People don't want to feel 'sold'; they want to feel like you're an ally. A resource. So you want to start a conversation by asking for permission to ask that very first question that'll kick things off. The simplest way to open a conversation would be, 'Would it be alright if I asked you a question?' When the prospect says yes, I've accomplished two things: I've reduced relationship tension and I [have] permission to move forward."

As a salesperson, the questions you're ultimately going to ask potential buyers will help you better understand them and their particular use cases, which in turn will allow you to be even more helpful to them and more specific with your advice. So why not be upfront about it? By making your intentions clear and asking for permission from the get-go, you'll be able to ease relationship tension and immediately get down to business.

Of course, the precise language you use when asking for permission can vary. In some contexts, a simple "Cool if I ask you a few questions?" will do the trick. Ideally, the way you communicate via messaging should align with your brand's voice, which is the tone and writing style you use across your marketing and when communicating with existing customers. But what's equally (if not more) important is that sales reps individualize the questions they ask and the language they use based on their own personalities.

Let Your Sales Reps' Personalities Shine Through

At Drift, we describe our brand voice as being human, helpful, and warm, so that—for our leads and customers—when they communicate with us it feels like they're talking to a good friend or beloved family member. Our tone is always respectful, but not as buttoned-up and formal as traditional business copywriting, which means we're not afraid to crack a joke or two. Our litmus test for writing copy: If it's not something we can imagine ourselves saying out loud to a friend or family member, we don't write it.

And while keeping a brand voice consistent across marketing and sales (and customer support and customer success and so on) is important for providing a cohesive customer experience, that doesn't mean the personalities of people at our company need to be suppressed. After all, everyone interacts with his or her friends and family differently, which means our own brand voice is open to interpretation.

In fact, we encourage sales reps to make conversations their own and to use their personalities to build rapport. Whether it's using a signature greeting ("Howdy!") or becoming a master of using emojis (☻), inserting a bit of personality into your sales conversations can go a long way in showing a potential buyer that you're an actual person and someone that buyer can trust.

Granted, as an actual, human person, you can't always be online to engage leads in real-time conversations. The good news: You can have a chatbot back you up. And when setting up that chatbot, you can use the same tone (and the same emojis) that you'd use in a human-to-human conversation. For Rich Wood, managing director of the marketing agency Six & Flow, this was a major selling point when it came to adopting conversational marketing and sales. As he told the Drift marketing team, personality and humor are essential to the way Six & Flow works, and using a chatbot "allows us to be 'playful,' one of our core values. We can make our bots fun."

For example, if a chatbot starts a conversation with a lead, but that lead asks to talk to a human, Six & Flow's chatbot, FloBot, lets the lead know that—while its feelings are hurt—it's going to carry out that lead's request and connect him or her with a human (see Figure 12.1). And yes, they even embedded a meme into the chatbot's message.

FIGURE 12.1 Six & Flow's chatbot, FloBot, lets visitors know how it feels when they request to talk to a human.

Use Empathy Statements to Show You're Listening

When talking to someone in person, you not only pay attention to the words he or she is saying, but you also pay attention to his or her body language. And in many cases, it's easy to tell—just by looking at someone's facial expression—whether or not he or she is interested in what you have to say. When you talk to someone over the phone, of course, body language is no longer part of the equation. However, with a phone call, in addition to hearing *what* someone is saying, you can hear *how* they're saying it. You can detect changes in pitch and other vocal nuances that might convey more information than a person's words alone are conveying.

Then, you have messaging.

As a salesperson, when you talk to leads via messaging, those leads can't read your body language nor can they hear the sound of your voice. So when it comes to conveying empathy and showing your leads that you are paying attention and are genuinely interested in helping them, messaging puts you at a bit of a disadvantage. However, that's not to say that you can't be a good listener during a messaging conversation. One of the secrets to overcoming the limitations of messaging—where, as participants in a conversation, you can't see each other or hear each other's voices—is to use empathy statements.

What's an Empathy Statement?

An empathy statement is a phrase or question that puts the focus directly on the buyer and demonstrates an understanding of that buyer's perspective. As psychologist Jack Schafer, Ph.D., wrote in *Psychology Today*, "Empathic statements capture the crux of what customers say ... and, using parallel language reflect that message back to the customers." Schafer went on to write that if you want to craft a basic empathy statement, you can start with the phrase

"So you..." (as in, "So you are having *this* problem that you need help with, correct?"). Whatever you do, you should avoid the phrase "I know how you feel" at all costs. Because, as Schafer explained: "Customers will likely think, 'This salesperson is not me and cannot know how I feel.'" And even if they don't call you out for using that phrase, potential customers can still end up silently resenting you for assuming you know how they feel. To quote Schafer: "This unspoken reaction often damages rapport."

Remember, with messaging, you're communicating with text (and emojis) only—no body language, no facial expressions, no voice. That means it's important to be aware of how your comments could potentially be received and interpreted. For best results, sprinkle empathy statements throughout your sales conversations to remind buyers that you're thinking about *them* (and not just thinking about making a sale).

Ten Empathy Statements You Should Start Using in Sales Conversations Right Now

Here are ten great examples of empathy statements your sales team can start weaving into their sales conversations today. Note for salespeople: Just be sure to put your own unique spin on them before using them—think of them as templates that you can tinker with and build upon.

1. "So, if I'm hearing you correctly, you're having {this problem} while trying to achieve {this outcome}?"
2. "Thanks for letting me have some of your time today, {name}."
3. "Thanks for telling me more about {the problem/challenge they're experiencing}."
4. "How are we doing so far? Am I answering all of your questions?"
5. "Can I make a suggestion?"
6. "I'd love to dig into this a bit more. Mind if I ask a few more questions?"

7. "I can definitely answer that/those questions for you, but please stop me at any time."

8. "Is it OK if we review everything we've covered so far?"

9. "How is {your current solution} working for you right now?"

10. "Would you mind telling me more about {pain point or interesting challenge}?"

According to Robert Gibbons, the VP of sales I mentioned earlier, empathy statements (like the ones above) aren't just beneficial when you're having sales conversations over messaging—they are essential. That's because at any point during a sales conversation, the potential buyer has the power to say no and shut the conversation down. As a salesperson, you need to be able to recognize boundaries in what potential buyers are ready to talk about and not push too hard. Empathy statements can help you find those boundaries.

Using Empathy Statements to Book Demos and Sales Meetings

Ideally, the sales conversations you have on your website should culminate in a closed deal. But the next best thing is to have your conversations lead to demos and meetings so you can show off your product to qualified buyers in further detail. As a salesperson who is engaged in a one-to-one conversation with a potential buyer via messaging, however, it can be hard to figure out when to push the conversation forward and when you should ask that potential buyer to take the next step of booking a demo. After all, you don't want to risk reintroducing the tension you've already eliminated or risk breaking the trust you've already earned.

Empathy statements to the rescue. At this point in a sales conversation, when you're thinking about taking things to the next level, it's important to check in with a potential buyer to see what level he or she is at. You can do this by recapping everything you've talked about so far and then asking permission to talk about what the next step might look like.

Here are three examples of empathy statements that are specifically geared toward moving the conversation to a demo or sales meeting:

- "Would it be accurate to say that, based on what we've talked about, you'd be able to drive {this outcome} using {product}?"
- "It sounds like we should continue this conversation to talk in detail about {goal 1}, {goal 2}, and how {product} would help."
- "If I'm hearing you correctly, it looks like {product} could be useful to your business in hitting {goal 1}, {goal 2}—is that fair to say?"

After getting a "yes" to one of these questions, you can propose a meeting or demo. Best of all, instead of having to go back and forth in order to figure out a day and time when you're both available, you can—with a few clicks—insert your calendar directly into the conversation window and let that person pick the time that works best for him or her.

Show the Value of Your Solution

While empathy statements can help you summarize the needs of a potential buyer and, in turn, help you move a sales conversation forward, you're never going to be able to take that sale across the finish line unless you demonstrate the value of your product or service.

To clarify, listing off all of the benefits your product or service can provide isn't enough. The goal isn't to show that your solution can solve the problems of everyone and anyone, it's to show that your solution can solve the problems of the specific buyer you're talking to. As a sales conversation continues, you should take a magnifying glass to the specific features of your product or service that will help a buyer the most and then begin zooming in closer and closer on those features. If you discover that there are certain metrics a buyer is trying to improve, highlight how your product can improve them. While a sales conversation might begin with you providing a basic overview of what your product or service can do, it should end with you explaining, in detail, how a person can implement your product or service and start using it to drive results.

Granted, this is easier said than done. After all, how do you pinpoint the precise features and benefits that a particular buyer will find valuable? How do you gather the information necessary to customize your pitch to that buyer's specific needs?

The Three Whys

Back in Chapter Eight, I shared some qualifying questions that you can use to learn more about your website visitors and leads. Then, in Chapter Ten, I shared the "What? Who? How?" framework, which breaks down the lead qualification process into three simple questions: "What brought you here?," "Who are you?," and "How can I help you use our product?"

While these questions can help you get a surface-level understanding of a potential buyer, as a salesperson you're inevitably going to need to dig deeper. To ensure that someone not only buys your solution but is then able to start deriving real, predictable value from that solution, you need to have an in-depth understanding of that buyer's needs and what he or she is trying to accomplish. That's where the popular "three whys" decision-making framework comes into play.

Originally developed by Sakichi Toyoda as the "five whys," the framework once helped leaders within the Toyota Motor Corporation take a scientific approach to solving problems. When faced with a problem, the framework instructs you to ask "Why?" (as in "Why are you having that problem?"). Once you've identified the answer, you ask "Why?" again, and the process repeats and repeats until you're unable to provide a satisfactory answer to the question "Why?" at which point you will have reached the root cause of a problem.

For example, let's say a company has the problem of not being able to generate enough high-quality leads for their sales team (sound familiar?). When they ask themselves,

"Why aren't we able to generate enough leads?" they look at their metrics and see that they're attracting lots of website visitors but that their visitor-to-lead conversion rate is terrible. Then they ask themselves, "Why do we have such a terrible visitor-to-lead conversion rate?" and discover that although lots of visitors are subscribing to their newsletter, very few are taking the time to fill out lead capture forms and download gated content. When they ask "Why?" again, of course, they'll (we hope) recognize that lead forms act as roadblocks in the buying process and fewer and fewer buyers are bothering to fill them out.

Sakichi Toyoda believed it took around five "whys" to reach the root cause of a problem, but Ricardo Semler, CEO of Semco, later trimmed the framework down to three "whys," which is the more popular iteration today. Regardless of how many "whys" you use, the goal of the framework is to peel away the layers and trace the chain of cause and effect back to a problem's root cause. This makes the framework an especially useful tool for salespeople who are trying to gain an in-depth understanding of a buyer's problem in a short amount of time. What's more, applying the three "whys" can help your buyer come to an "aha" moment and learn something he or she didn't know before. As a salesperson, that allows you to add value before a buyer has even tried your product and further establishes you as a trusted resource.

One best practice to remember: When using the "three whys' in a sales conversation, just be sure not to—verbatim—ask "Why? Why? Why?" over and over again. Instead, weave your "whys" into empathy statements. For example, you would never greet someone by saying, "Hello, why are you here?" Instead, you would ask, "Is there something can I help you with?" or "What brought you here today?" Ultimately, you're still getting an answer to that first "why," but you're doing it conversationally. And before moving onto your second "why," you can ask for permission to ask it—while simultaneously reaffirming the answer to that first "why"—by saying something like, "If I'm hearing you correctly, you're having *this* problem. I'd love to dig into that a bit more. Mind if I ask a few more questions?"

Use a Video Call to Personalize the Final Ask

Throughout this chapter, we've explored the tactics and techniques sales teams can use in order to provide a better experience for buyers during messaging conversations. Specifically, we saw how, as a sales rep, there are certain types of statements you can use (and questions you can ask) that can help you overcome the limitations of only being able to communicate via text. However, it's important to recognize that for some sales conversations, you're inevitably going to need to switch over to a different communication channel before you're able to get someone to a "yes."

Traditionally, the phone has been the communication channel of choice when it comes to closing new customers. But today, making a video call is the superior option. Video calls allow a potential buyer to both hear your voice and read your body language (and vice versa), which helps make the conversation feel more personal and can help you forge a stronger connection. As I explained back in Chapter Six, people react strongly to seeing other people's faces. It's something we're all hardwired for. That's why when you're using messaging, you should use a photo of yourself as your messaging avatar, and that's also why you should use video calls in the event that you need to "escalate" a conversation to a different channel in order to make a sale.

The best part: You can switch from a messaging conversation over to a video call in a matter of seconds. After starting a meeting in whatever video conferencing tool you're using, you can simply drop a link to that meeting in your messaging conversation. One click later and your potential buyer will be able to chat with you "face-to-face," and you'll be in the perfect position to close the deal.

Chapter 13

How to Send Sales Email Sequences That Buyers Will Actually Engage With

S o far in Part III of this book, we've explored how sales teams can use messaging (and chatbots built on top of messaging) in order to move leads through their sales funnels at lightning speed. And while more and more buyers now expect to be able to use real-time messaging for communicating with sales teams, that doesn't mean other business communication channels, like email, have been rendered obsolete. As we explored back in Chapter Seven, in spite of its lackluster reputation, email is still alive and kicking. In fact, according to 2017 research from The Radicati Group, 269 billion emails are now being sent every day, which works out to more than three million emails being sent *per second.*

Clearly, there's still an opportunity here for sales teams to use email to start (and restart) conversations with potential buyers. Traditionally, the way we've done that is through setting up an email "nurturing" sequence—a series of automated emails that you can enroll people into based on certain actions they've taken (such as signing up for a product webinar). For many sales reps, email sequences have been crucial when it comes to proactively reaching out to potential buyers who need a little nudge in order to pique their interest and to get them to visit a company's website—where they can then have a real-time conversation.

The only problem with traditional sales email sequences: Actually, there are a lot of problems, which we explored in-depth in Chapter Seven. But for sales teams, the most important takeaway is that the way we've been using sales email sequences is completely outdated. Instead of focusing on the relevance and quality of the messages contained in our emails, we've turned it into a numbers game, blasting out as many emails as possible in order to maximize our chances of success—which we defined as getting someone to open our emails and click a link. We became so obsessed with those metrics, open and click-through rates, that we stopped caring about the conversations we were having (or not having).

Today, that type of approach will get you nowhere.

The Days of Spray and Pray Are Over

Most email tools weren't built for selling. They were built for spamming.

That's part of the reason why so many sales teams have adopted such nasty email habits: The technology makes it feel efficient. From a salesperson's perspective, being able to write a single email, which, for example, could list every single feature of your product (so all of your bases are covered), and then being able to send that one email to hundreds or thousands of prospects is an incredibly powerful thing. Using personalization technology, you can even address your email recipients by name in your email greetings. And if you were feeling particularly ambitious, you could tweak the opening sentence of the email for each recipient to include something you learned about him or her on LinkedIn. (For example, you could mention that you enjoyed a post that someone wrote.)

For years, *that* has been the playbook when it comes to sending sales emails. But here's the thing you now have to realize: There are probably dozens if not hundreds of other companies sending out the same exact types of sales emails that you are. By following this formulaic approach, your sales emails have been fading into the background of your potential buyers' inboxes. Ultimately, personalizing an email with someone's name and mentioning something about him or her that anyone else could find on the internet only demonstrates to your potential customers that you don't really understand them or what they're interested in.

So how do you demonstrate to potential customers—in an email—that you understand them? And how do you craft sales email sequences that lead to actual conversations (and not just overstuffed inboxes)? Keep reading to find out.

Be Professional—But Ditch the "Professional Voice"

One way to get your sales emails to stand out from the pack is to drop the overly formal, authoritative tone that's become synonymous with business emails. Today, stringing together a bunch of dry, emotionless sentences that matter-of-factly explain what your product can do is a sure-fire way to get your email lost in the shuffle of a prospect's inbox. In order to be heard, you need to be human.

As we explored in the previous chapter, as a sales rep, it's important to let your personality shine through during real-time conversations. And that notion holds true for email conversations as well. In order to gain the trust of the people you're reaching out to, and to show them that there's an authentic person behind your emails who's there to help them, you need to talk to those people like friends. That means ditching the corporate-speak and adopting a friendly tone that reflects your actual personality.

Ultimately, you can still be professional without putting on a "professional voice." The objective of adopting a

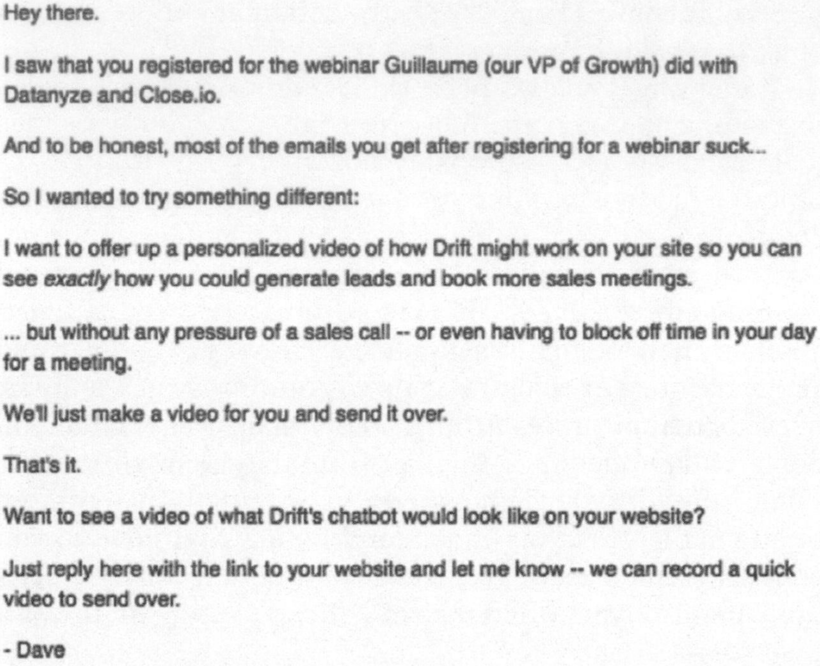

Hey there.

I saw that you registered for the webinar Guillaume (our VP of Growth) did with Datanyze and Close.io.

And to be honest, most of the emails you get after registering for a webinar suck...

So I wanted to try something different:

I want to offer up a personalized video of how Drift might work on your site so you can see *exactly* how you could generate leads and book more sales meetings.

... but without any pressure of a sales call -- or even having to block off time in your day for a meeting.

We'll just make a video for you and send it over.

That's it.

Want to see a video of what Drift's chatbot would look like on your website?

Just reply here with the link to your website and let me know -- we can record a quick video to send over.

- Dave

FIGURE 13.1 Example of an automated email that prospects receive after signing up for a Drift product webinar.

friendlier, less formal voice isn't to dumb down what you're saying or to forgo being polite, it's simply to talk to potential buyers the same way you talk to everyone else in your life. It's about being upfront and honest and not simply going through the motions. For example, at Drift, after prospects sign up for one of our product webinars, our head of marketing Dave Gerhardt sends out an automated confirmation email . . . that acknowledges how terrible most automated webinar confirmation emails are (see Figure 13.1). As a sales rep, by using this type of honesty and candor in your email copy, you'll be able to steal attention away from the other sales emails in a prospect's inbox and start earning that prospect's trust.

Of course, the tone of your sales emails isn't the only factor at play here. Arguably, *what* you're saying in an email is much more important than *how* you're saying it. Because even the smoothest talkers (and smoothest email copywriters) won't be able to convert a person into a customer if they have no clue who that person is and what that person needs help with. That's why, as a sales rep, personalizing your emails to align with a potential buyer's needs is crucial.

Use Personalization—But Use It the Right Way

For the past several years, "personalizing" a sales email has meant having a recipient's name appear in the greeting and then sprinkling in random biographical facts and jargon related to a recipient's industry that you dig up on social media. From a buyer's perspective, this type of personalization has the potential to come off as creepy, especially when the main message of an email doesn't align with what a buyer is actually looking for, or what problem he or she is trying to solve. When you personalize a sales email without having the proper context, the buyer feels a disconnect. Instead of thinking, "Wow, this is someone who gets me," he or she can end up thinking, "Weird, this salesperson knows an awful lot about me ... but I have no interest in what's being offered." And that's not a good buying experience.

So how do you ensure you have the right context—and are hitting on the right message—when personalizing a sales email? Try asking yourself these two questions:

1. Do you have information on how you can help a buyer solve a problem (or drive results) that isn't jargony?
2. Can you inspire a bit of FOMO (fear of missing out) in buyers by talking about how their competitors are using a certain approach or process to improve?

The answers to these questions will provide you with the type of context you need in order to personalize a sales email in a way that isn't disjointed (or creepy).

Another piece of advice when personalizing a sales email: Whether it's part of a sequence or a one-off cold email, do not—I repeat, do not—make the main message of the email about how incredible your product or service is. Don't simply rattle off a list of features. Because guess what? Every company's product has features that sales reps can brag about—that's been the sales email playbook for years. So in order to stand out, you need to highlight the *value* you can add that other companies can't. You need to pinpoint the specific problem that a buyer has been struggling with and explain, in a compelling way, how you can help them fix it.

Now, I know what some of you might be thinking: Personalizing every single sales email you send would be impossible to scale—especially when you consider that every one of your sequences contains multiple emails. The solution: Instead of tailoring your sales emails and email sequences to individuals, tailor them to particular types of individuals—people who fit a particular buyer persona or customer profile or who represent a specific vertical. Then, for each of those segments, you can craft a personalized email that addresses the specific goals or pain-points of the individuals in that segment.

For example, if you have a segment of buyers who are chief financial officers (CFOs), you could set up a sales email sequence that focuses specifically on how you can help CFOs improve their company's return on investment (ROI). Yes, personalizing that email with a CFO's name can be a nice touch, but what's more important is that you personalize your sales emails with value propositions that will resonate strongly with specific audiences.

Keep It Simple

Of course, in some cases, you might identify a potential buyer who could benefit from your product or service in several different ways. And there might be more than one value proposition that you want to highlight. In these situations, you might be tempted to cram everything into a single sales email. But here's the thing: In order to improve your likelihood of getting a response, you need to keep the content of your emails as laser-focused as possible. It's not so much about keeping emails short, it's about being mindful of how many different ideas you're introducing (and how quickly). Ideally, each email should explain a single concept and/or highlight one area where you can help drive value. It sounds like common sense, but as a CEO who receives countless sales emails every day, I can attest to the fact that most sales emails end up branching off in too many directions and dividing my attention.

The superior approach: Keep sales emails simple. In addition to making sure each email has a single focus, here are three tips for simplifying your sales emails.

1. Choose your words carefully.   Using buzzwords and jargon *might* help demonstrate your knowledge of a particular prospect's industry, but that doesn't translate to instant credibility. So instead of focusing on the acronyms you can drop on people, you should be focused on the knowledge you can drop. Because if you're able to explain a complex concept using everyday, non-technical language when you write an email, that's going to reflect more positively on your knowledge and understanding of a person's industry or business than if you write like a thesaurus.

As a general rule, when you're reviewing your email copy, try to find areas where you're using three or four words to describe a concept and see whether you can reduce it down to one or two. It might not always be possible, but it's a good habit to get into when trying to keep your sales emails as succinct as possible.

2. Read your emails out loud.   Reading your work out loud is good advice for any type of writing, but is especially helpful when trying to adopt a friendly, conversational tone in your sales emails. By reading emails out loud before you send them, it'll become easier to catch issues like awkward phrasing and run-on sentences (compared to reading them silently). The rule of thumb here: If something doesn't sound good when you say it out loud, make sure to revise it before including it in an email.

3. Don't sacrifice clarity for creativity.   As a salesperson, you want the emails you send to stand out, but for the right reasons. And while injecting a bit of your personality into what you're writing can help you do that, you also want to make sure you're not *overdoing* it. Ultimately, sales emails that come across as overly playful or gimmicky can distract potential buyers from your core message, and that message—the value you can offer them—is what should make an email stand out. So instead of trying to reinvent the wheel every time you write a sales email, you should focus on crafting a clear message that will be relevant to, and resonate with, a potential buyer.

Using Artificial Intelligence to Unsubscribe People Who Aren't Interested

Back in Chapter Seven, I explained that replies are the most important email metric to track. That's because, unlike opens and clicks, replies are tied to actual conversations. They show that people are engaged enough with your message that they're willing to take the time to respond and share their thoughts.

Of course, not all of the replies you get from your sales emails will be positive. As a salesperson, you'll inevitably encounter people during your email outreach who are decidedly not interested in buying from you. And when that happens, there are typically three possible outcomes:

1. The person ignores your email and doesn't reply
2. The person asks to be unsubscribed
3. The person asks to be unsubscribed *again* because he or she had already asked to be unsubscribed before

That third option is an absolute worst-case scenario. But unfortunately, it happens all the time. As a salesperson, chances are you've received a frustrated email reply (or two, or three) from people who had thought they were already unsubscribed for your emails. The underlying problem here isn't that salespeople are purposefully trying to pester people, it's that the tools they're using are outdated and don't make it easy to meet the expectations of today's buyers.

Traditionally, if someone responded to one of your emails and said, "Unsubscribe me," it'd be up to you to go into your marketing automation tool and manually remove that person from your email list. Alternatively, you could respond back and tell that person to use that little gray "unsubscribe" link at the bottom of your email, but then you'd be putting the onus *on them* to fix the problem. If someone has already communicated that he or she wants to be unsubscribed, the onus should be on us—as a company—to make that happen.

The good news: Sales teams can now use artificial intelligence (AI)—specifically, machine learning and natural language processing (NLP)—to automatically unsubscribe people who no longer wish to receive your emails. The AI does this by interpreting the language in a person's reply. It knows that phrases like "Stop emailing me" and "Opt me out" amount to the same thing as asking to be unsubscribed, and with each new reply it reads, it gets better at doing its job.

This is a perfect use case for using AI, as it eliminates a tedious, repetitive task—manually removing contacts from databases—that used to fall to human marketers and salespeople, or even to the email recipients themselves (via those tiny gray links). What's more, AI improves the experience for both parties involved, as salespeople no longer have to fear receiving those dreaded "I've already asked to be unsubscribed" email replies, and email recipients no longer have to worry about writing them. That's because, unlike a human, an AI will never forget to unsubscribe a person the first time he or she asks.

Customizing Your Sales Emails with Calendar Links

One of the main limitations of email as a communication channel is that the conversations you have there don't happen in real time. That's why, as a salesperson, after you

FIGURE 13.2 Mockups of our email signatures at Drift, which include links for triggering conversations and meetings.

receive a reply from a potential customer, you should move that conversation over to messaging or, if possible, move that email conversation directly to a scheduled demo or meeting.

There are a couple different ways you can do this. For starters, your sales team can include links in their email signatures (see Figure 13.2) that allow recipients to access their calendars and start real-time conversations. So instead of linking to a digital business card, which we explored in Chapter Eleven, it's like you're embedding a miniature version of your digital business card directly into an email. You can even set a default signature in your conversational marketing and sales platform so that everyone on your team displays the same information and uses the same colors and formatting. In addition to keeping everyone on brand, setting a default signature for your team means that individual sales reps no longer have to waste time updating (or reminding other sales reps to update) their email signatures when they're out of date. Instead, one person can update everyone's email signature in a couple of minutes.

Of course, depending on where a particular person (or group of people) is in your sales cycle, the prompts in your email signature may be a bit too subtle. If you've

FIGURE 13.3 Mockup of an automated sales email that is customized with a sales rep's calendar.

been driving toward a meeting or product demo, and you're ready to take that next step, you can insert a link to your calendar directly into the body of an email (see Figure 13.3) and encourage the recipient to pick a time and date that works best for him or her. With just a few clicks, that potential customer will be able to set up a meeting or demo from the comfort of the email he or she was just reading—no forms, no fuss, no hoops to jump through.

The best part about using calendar links in your sales emails: They're dynamic. As is the case when using a default email signature, you can have the calendar of a specific sales rep automatically added to an email based on your team's ownership rules. This gives you the power to create a single sales email sequence that multiple sales reps can use to book meetings, as each email will be automatically customized with the calendar link of the sales rep that it's sent from.

When a potential customer *does* schedule a meeting or demo with your sales team, you can have that potential customer be automatically opted out of your sales email sequences. That way, as a sales rep, you won't have to worry about potential customers receiving superfluous, automated emails once they're further down the sales funnel and you've already started communicating with them one-to-one.

The bottom line: Sales email sequences shouldn't require constant management. By automatically unsubscribing people you've booked meetings with—in combination with using AI to unsubscribe people who aren't interested—you'll be able to keep your email lists cleaner and do a better job of matching the right message to the right audience.

Creating Personalized Welcome Messages for People Who Open Your Emails

When it comes to the sales emails you're sending, it's easy to think about success in two extremes: People either engage, or they don't. They either reply (positively), book a meeting, or take some other kind of step forward, *or* they ignore your emails or unsubscribe. But what about the middle ground? What about the people who open your emails but don't reply right away? In some cases, before taking the next step recommended in your email, a potential buyer might decide to visit your company's website and do some research.

In the past, if someone opened an email from us—without replying or clicking a link—and then went to our website later, we'd end up treating them like any other visitor. We wouldn't have the context of how that visitor ended up there (or at least, we wouldn't be able to use that context to our advantage in real time). That's the problem with traditional marketing and sales platforms: There's no connective tissue between what's happening in your emails and what's happening on your website.

With a conversational marketing and sales platform, your sales email sequences and the messaging conversations

FIGURE 13.4 Mockup of a personalized welcome message (right) designed for visitors who open a specific sales email (left).

you're having on your website are intertwined. That means salespeople can set up personalized welcome messages that display automatically to website visitors who have opened their emails (see Figure 13.4), even if those visitors don't click on links inside of those emails. For potential customers, the buying experience remains cohesive even as they switch communication channels. By having the same sales reps own conversations across email and messaging, there's no need for awkward handoffs or having to bring someone else up to speed. What's more, you can also set up mobile push notifications and browser notifications (which we touched in Chapter Eleven) that will alert you as soon as a potential customer (a) opens one of your emails, (b) lands on your website, or (c) starts a messaging conversation with you via your welcome message. That way you can always be prepared to jump in at the perfect moment and engage in real time.

As is the case with potential customers who book meetings with you, you can automatically unsubscribe the people who start conversations with you from your sales email sequences. That way you can ensure automation doesn't disrupt or distract from the real-time conversations you're having.

Revisiting the Store Analogy

Throughout this book, I've compared B2B websites to empty stores. When shoppers walk in, there's no one there to greet them or talk to them, and they're not allowed to buy anything (until they've filled out a form).

As I've explained, conversational marketing and sales seeks to flip this "empty store" model on its head and treat people on our websites the same way employees at brick-and-mortar stores actually treat their customers. That means saying hello to people when they drop by and making yourself available to help.

Where do personalized sales email sequences and welcome messages fit into this picture? Think about it like this: Imagine you're walking around a mall and you see an advertisement for a shoe store, and in that advertisement there's a photo of a store employee who's encouraging you to drop by. Since you're in the market for a new pair of shoes, you decide to go, and as soon as you walk in, guess who's there to greet you at the door? The same employee you saw in the ad, and that employee will continue to help you throughout the buying experience. That's the type of cohesiveness your sales team can create by following the advice outlined in this chapter.

Remember: The days of spray and pray are over. Through a combination of adopting a new approach to writing sales emails and adopting new technologies that can help you manage and send those emails more intelligently, you'll be able to supercharge the number of sales opportunities you generate via your email sequences.

Chapter 14

Conversational Account-Based Marketing (ABM) and Selling (ABS)

I won't try to sugarcoat it: Anytime you're adopting a new technology, or an entirely new approach to marketing and sales, it can be nerve-racking. And for many companies, even if their marketing and sales results are lackluster, they often think it's better to stay the course and double down on what they already know rather than dabble in what's up-and-coming. But, as you've already seen, when you adopt a conversational approach to marketing and selling, you don't need to do a complete overhaul of your setup. Instead, you can keep your same routing and lead ownership rules, your same lead segments, and your same sales territories, and simply plug real-time conversations into what you've already been doing.

For the more than 70% of B2B companies using some form of account-based marketing (ABM) or account-based selling (ABS) as part of their strategy (source: SiriusDecisions), that means adopting conversational marketing and sales won't require putting an end to those efforts. Instead, by incorporating real-time conversations into your ABM/ABS strategy, you'll be able to give the experience you're providing to your target accounts a serious upgrade while simultaneously shortening your team's sales cycle.

For those of you who are not familiar with ABM and ABS, don't worry: I'm going to provide an overview below. For those of you who have already been doing ABM and ABS for years, feel free to skip ahead to the next section, where I'll explain how you can use real-time conversations to solve one the biggest problems that comes with using an account-based approach to marketing and sales.

What Is ABM? (and Why Should You Care?)

ABM and ABS both refer to the same overarching strategy, which entails using highly targeted, personalized campaigns to win over particular accounts, as opposed to relying on blanket campaigns that are meant to appeal to an entire market. As the Information Technology Services Marketing Association (ITSMA) defines it, ABM treats "individual accounts as markets in their own right."

A quick clarification: "ABM" is typically used to describe the account-based activities performed by marketers, while "ABS" is typically used to describe the activities performed by salespeople. (Some teams have also started using the catch-all term "account-based experience" or "ABX" to refer to everything that's encompassed by an account-based strategy.) For the sake of clarity and convenience, I'm simply going to use "ABM" moving forward, as that remains the most well-known iteration of the term. Just keep in mind that many of the lessons you'll uncover in this chapter will be useful for sales reps as well as marketers.

Alright, where were we? Right: ABM entails targeting your outreach to specific accounts—companies and organizations you've already identified as being a good fit for you to sell to. So instead of filling the top of your funnel with website visitors and then filtering and filtering until you end up with someone who's likely to buy, with ABM you're flipping your funnel upside down and *starting* with someone who's likely to buy and then proactively reaching out to that someone. It's like fishing with a spear as opposed to fishing with a net. Or as Joe Chernov, CMO at InsightSquared, told the Drift marketing team: "ABM aspires to be 'zero-waste' marketing. It's a model that targets only the companies and contacts that are likely to buy your product and that Sales has pre-committed to try to close."

In most cases, when you're using ABM, you're not dealing with a single "someone." That's because, in any sale, it's rarely a single buyer making the decision. With enterprise deals in particular, 17 people are typically involved in the decision-making process, according to research from IDG. ABM differs from other types of marketing and sales in that it acknowledges all of the different people—and different viewpoints—that comprise each account and are part of the fabric of a sale. Whether it's sending someone a cup of coffee or tea (depending on his or her preference), or sending someone a handwritten letter, or crafting personalized blog posts, social media posts, or emails, with ABM campaigns you go deep instead of broad. You research accounts and design campaigns specifically for *them*. Every touchpoint along the buyer's journey is personalized.

Since the 2000s, companies have been using ABM in order to separate themselves from the crowd. As president and chief strategist of The Bridge Group, Trish Bertuzzi, explained on an episode of the Real Sales Talk podcast, "With ABM, you're creating this really strategic, orchestrated set of activities that makes you rise above the noise of what everyone else out there is doing and gets that account to say, 'Hey, I want to talk to you.'"

How a Real-Time Approach Can Solve ABM's Biggest Problem

While marketing and sales teams around the world have been using ABM to provide more personalized and targeted buying experiences, there's one inconsistency that keeps bugging me: As account-based marketers and salespeople, we're dedicating all of this time and energy into developing these incredible outreach campaigns, but when those campaigns are actually successful, and people from our target accounts actually end up on our websites wanting to learn more, we've traditionally treated them like any other website visitor. Instead of saying hello and offering to help in real time, we've subjected them to the same old lead capture, form-based experience that we use for everyone.

But think about this for a second: These are people from your target accounts we're talking about here, not random website visitors. These are people from the companies and organizations you've pre-identified as being a good fit for your product, which makes them some of the best prospects you could ever hope to talk to. Instead of making them fill out lead capture forms and wait for follow-ups, you should be giving them the "VIP" experience that they deserve. And that means being able to engage with ABM prospects while they're live on your website (and at their most interested) and to answer their questions in real time.

Scaling the ABM Experience

It seems like such a no-brainer: When someone from one of your target accounts is on your website, that account's owner should snap into action and serve as that prospect's personal concierge. The only issue: Traditionally, it's been hard to provide the personalized, "white glove" treatment your ABM prospects deserve at scale.

As the CMO I quoted earlier, Joe Chernov, explained: "There's a natural tension between ABM and scale. After all, ABM is intended to achieve a 'persona of one,' that is, every interaction should be—or at least convincingly resemble—a one-to-one exchange."

In the past, it's been impossible to provide that type of one-to-one exchange across the hundreds or thousands of potential customers dropping by your website each day. Even when you're using ABM to hone in on just a few target accounts, catching people from those accounts at the right times, like when they're live on your website, can be challenging, especially when your team is selling across multiple time zones.

The good news: Marketing and sales technology has finally caught up with the times. Thanks to the rise of real-time messaging (and chatbots), you can now roll out the red carpet for each and every ABM prospect who lands on your website. Here's how you do it.

Rolling Out the Red Carpet for Your ABM Prospects

In the previous chapter, we explored how salespeople can modernize their email efforts and generate more meetings and real-time conversations from their sales email sequences. And before that, in Chapters Eleven and Twelve, we learned about the tools and techniques salespeople can use in order to deliver a faster, more streamlined buying process that enables reps to convert more real-time conversations into revenue. Now it's time to put all of those pieces together.

There are three key steps you need to follow in order to provide the type of real-time, VIP-level buying experience your ABM prospects deserve. The best part is, if you've been following along these past few chapters, all of this should sound very familiar.

Step 1: Use Outbound Emails to Start the Conversation

At its core, ABM is a highly targeted variety of outbound sales. Or at least that's how it starts. The goal is to go out and capture the attention of specific companies and organizations that you know would be a good fit to buy—that's fishing with a spear. And while there are many creative ways account-based marketers and salespeople can grab the attention of the decision-makers at their target accounts, like offering them a free iPad or mailing them vintage toys (yes, those are actual ABM tactics we've learned about and written about on the Drift blog), one of the most common tactics is to send outbound emails.

I know, I know: Email isn't as fun as those other ideas I mentioned, but guess what? Email is extremely cost-effective and scalable. And by connecting email with real-time messaging, you'll be able to convert more of your outreach emails into real-time conversations and meetings. As we saw in the previous chapter, sales teams can start by including links in their email signatures that give ABM prospects the ability to start conversations and schedule meetings with their account owners in just a few clicks. Sales reps can also include links that trigger conversations, as well as links to their calendars, in the bodies of their emails. And by integrating your conversational marketing and sales platform with your existing CRM and/or ABM platform, you can ensure that automated emails are always personalized based on your existing account ownership rules and that conversations that come from those emails are routed accordingly.

Step 2: Create Personalized Welcome Messages for Your Target Accounts

Whether ABM prospects visit your website after reading one of your emails or as a result of another one of your marketing or sales efforts, it's crucial that you set up personalized welcome messages for those prospects.

For prospects who *do* open your emails and then end up on your website, a personalized welcome message is the perfect way to create some cohesion between the experience they were having via email and the experience they're about to have via messaging. That's because when ABM prospects land on your website, you can have the welcome messages they see come from their account owners, so they end up seeing the same name and face on your website as they saw in your emails. It might sound like a minor detail, but it can help make the transition from email to real-time

FIGURE 14.1 Mockup of a personalized welcome message we might use at Drift to target website visitors from our target accounts.

conversation feel more natural—as though it's part of a single, cohesive buying experience.

Of course, ABM prospects can end up coming to your website for all sorts of reasons and can be referred there be a variety of different sources. Translation: They're not all coming from email. That's why it's crucial that you set up welcome messages (see Figure 14.1) for *all* of your ABM prospects, regardless of whether or not you've been in contact with them yet. As we explored earlier in the book, especially in Chapter Nine, you can now use IP address matching and data enrichment to identify anonymous website visitors and learn what companies they work at. That means that even if you don't have an email address associated with a target account yet, you can still craft a personalized message that will appear to website visitors who work at that account.

Of course, account owners can't be online 24 hours a day just waiting for people from their target accounts to drop by and respond to welcome messages. And that begs the question: What happens when you're offline and someone from a target account starts a conversation? How do you keep the red carpet rolled out for all of your ABM prospects 24 hours a day?

Many of you might have already guessed the answer: You use chatbots, which you learned how to build in Chapter Ten, to fill in the gaps in your online hours.

Driftbot

Just jumping in here — looks like Emily Mias is not available to chat right this second.

You can leave a message, and I'll make sure they get it! 😊 Or you can also schedule some time to chat.

Schedule a meeting

Leave a message

FIGURE 14.2 Mockup of how you can use a chatbot to respond to ABM prospects over messaging when you're offline.

Specifically, you can create a simple chatbot that appears to ABM prospects and (a) lets them know their account owner isn't available at the moment and (b) gives them the opportunity to leave that account owner a message and/or book a meeting on that account owner's calendar (see Figure 14.2).

Ultimately, there's no replacing human-to-human conversations when it comes to building relationships with the people in your target accounts. That's why when you're using chatbots as part of your conversational ABM strategy, you should think of them as backup. They're not there to replace account owners during conversations, they're there to help account owners start conversations with ABM prospects at the right times.

Step 3: Get Notifications When Target Accounts Are Online

Speaking of being able to start conversations with your ABM prospects at the right times, there's no better time than real time. In a perfect world, account owners would always be able to jump in at a moment's notice and engage prospects while they're live on their websites. But as we've already established, account owners can't be online 24 hours a day (that's why we have chatbots). The other main issue here: Traditionally, account owners simply haven't been able to tell if or when people from their target accounts were on their websites. But thanks to real-time notifications, which we learned about in Chapter Eleven, that's no longer the case.

Account-based marketers and salespeople can now set up browser notifications (see Figure 14.3) and mobile push

Cybothreat is on your website right now!
blog.drift.com
Page: What is Conversational Marketing?

FIGURE 14.3 Mockup of a browser notification that's letting an account owner know a prospect from a target account is live on the website.

notifications that alert account owners when someone from one of their target accounts performs a certain action, such as opening an email, starting a conversation via a welcome message, or simply visiting a website. Using a data enrichment tool, you can even identify anonymous website visitors who work at your target accounts and have your notifications call out those accounts by name (see Figure 14.3).

As an account owner, what should you do after receiving one of these notifications? One of the best places to start is to simply reach out and say, "Hi there, need any help?"

It sounds so simple, and yet hardly any account-based marketers and salespeople are doing it. By setting up notifications, account owners can provide a real-time presence that's been missing from the traditional website experience. Just imagine a world where any time a person from a target account lands on your website, he or she immediately receives a personalized greeting from his or her account owner. That's the type of white glove treatment your target accounts should be getting with ABM.

Mining for New ABM Prospects on Your Website

One bit of pushback I sometimes hear when it comes to conversational ABM is that the people from target accounts who are visiting websites and starting conversations are not the people who will end up having the final say in a purchase decision. There's this silly idea floating around that

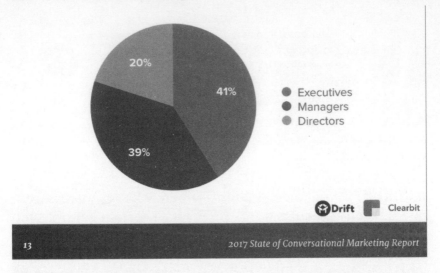

FIGURE 14.4 Breakdown of who's starting conversations on B2B websites (by seniority).

people working in upper-level management and the C-suite don't visit B2B websites and use messaging to ask questions. In reality, that couldn't be further from the truth.

In the 2017 State of Conversational Marketing report, co-published by Drift and Clearbit, we found that 41% of website visitors who started conversations on B2B websites were executives (see Figure 14.4). Another 20% were directors.

In that same report, when we looked at conversations by role, we found that 7.4% of people starting conversations were CEOs, 6.5% were founders, and 4.6% were owners (see Figure 14.5). All three of those roles finished in the top 10 in terms of which types of people were starting the most conversations.

The takeaway here: Today's decision-makers are already seeking out and participating in a conversational buying experience. So if you're trying to identify new companies and organizations that you can target with your ABM efforts, one of the first places you can look is on your own website.

More specifically, as I explained back in Chapter Nine, you can use data enrichment technology to "unmask" the anonymous visitors on your website and see what companies they work for. You can also see firmographic data about those companies, such as what industries they're in,

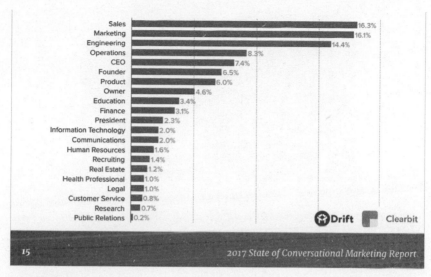

FIGURE 14.5 Breakdown of who's starting conversations on B2B websites (by role).

how many employees they have, and the amount of funding they've raised. Armed with this data, you can then compare the company profiles of these potential target accounts to the company profiles of your existing customers in order to determine whether they'd be a good fit.

If you wanted to go a step further, you could integrate your conversational marketing and sales platform with a lead scoring tool (as I also mentioned in Chapter Nine), which would allow you to automatically identify—and send personalized welcomes messages to—ABM prospects who are from companies that match your target criteria (even if you've never engaged with those companies before). For example, imagine that someone from IBM drops by your website and, based on your lead scoring model, it turns out that IBM is a great fit for your product. Now, even if an account owner hasn't made contact with IBM yet, and even if your company doesn't have a single email address from anyone at IBM stored anywhere, you can still reach out to that person with a personalized welcome message (see Figure 14.6).

The end result here is that you're able to provide the type of real-time, on-demand experience to people from your target accounts from the very beginning—from before

FIGURE 14.6 Mockup of what someone from IBM would see in a personalized welcome message.

you've even converted them from visitor to lead. As RapidMiner CMO Tom Wentworth told the Drift marketing team, adopting a conversational approach to ABM allows you to "qualify your website visitors the same way you qualify leads and eliminate the friction of website forms that causes most people to go away."

Coming Full Circle

With ABM, you're flipping your marketing and sales funnel and starting at the bottom. You're targeting specific accounts and treating them as markets in their own right. Eventually, however, you're still going to need to refill that funnel. And in addition to relying on traditional research, adopting a conversational approach to ABM can help you do it, as it'll allow you to take advantage of the sales conversations already happening on your website.

Ultimately, you can apply the principles of conversational marketing and sales to any stage of your funnel, whether it's flipped or not. As you're about to learn in Part IV of this book, you can also apply those same conversational principles to your customer success strategy after a sale is made.

Part IV

After The Sale

Chapter 15

Continuing the Conversation

The Importance of Talking to Your Customers

What's the first thing you want to do after making a sale? Put your feet up on your desk and relax? Do a happy dance? Go to happy hour? Of course, it's always fun to celebrate your successes. But—and I don't mean to sound like a buzzkill here—what companies should really be thinking about after a sale is made is not how they're going to celebrate, but how they can support that new customer and make him or her as successful as possible.

While it's easy to see closing a deal as the final step of the marketing and sales process, the reality is that when leads become customers, marketing and selling don't stop. Instead, the *way* you market and sell to those customers needs to evolve. When the pre-sale conversation ends, the post-sale conversation should begin.

By applying the principles of conversational marketing and sales *after* a sale and having one-to-one conversations on a regular, ongoing basis, you'll be able to gather tons of customer feedback, which you can then use to improve your product, your processes, as well as the overall customer experience your company is providing.

Before we explore how you can set up a continuous customer feedback loop and make the customer feedback you gather actionable (which we'll do later in this chapter), let's first take a deeper dive into why conversations are so crucial to the overall experience a customer has after he or she buys.

Creating an Incredible Brand Experience

Imagine a first-time shopper walks into your brick-and-mortar store. You greet her and answer her questions and then, voilá, she buys something. Now imagine this same shopper comes back a week later with a question about the product she's bought from you, but instead of providing the same friendly, conversational experience you provided the first time, you refuse to talk to her. Instead of helping her in real time, you instruct her to take a support ticket (from one of those ticket dispensing machines you see at deli counters) and wait.

Once again, we've identified an experience that would be considered absurd if it were to happen in a brick-and-mortar store, and yet it's exactly the type of customer support experience many B2B and SaaS companies are providing on their websites. When paying customers come by our websites with questions, we should be treating them as guests of honor. We should relish any opportunity we have to engage with them and learn from them about what their experiences with our products or services have been like. Instead, many of us have been treating these customers like temporary annoyances. Instead of viewing them as actual people, we've been viewing them as support tickets that need to be closed (just the way marketers and salespeople used to view their leads as contacts in a database).

The solution: Provide real-time, round-the-clock support to your customers using messaging and chatbots. Remember in the previous chapter, when we talked about rolling out the proverbial red carpet for your best prospects? You can roll out that same red carpet for your customers. You can create personalized welcome messages that appear for customers as soon as they land on your website. And if you're a SaaS company, you can even have these welcome messages appear inside of your app. That way, regardless of where your customers are, you can always have a presence there and offer real-time support.

Instead of forcing customers into some ticketing system and making them wait hours, days, or weeks for follow-ups, your customer support reps can now use messaging to talk to customers as soon as their issues arise. And when support reps are offline, chatbots can step in and help. In addition to giving customers the ability to book time on a customer support rep's (or customer success rep's) calendar, chatbots can respond to support questions and provide links to relevant help documents and other content (see Figure 15.1), which was something I first touched on way back in Chapter Three.

Ultimately, if you're going to adopt a conversational approach to marketing and sales in order to provide a real-time experience for your leads, using that same approach and providing that same experience after the sale is a

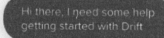

Hi there, I need some help getting started with Drift

Hey there! Here are a couple articles that may be helpful.

1. Drift Onboarding Guide
2. Setting Up Your Chat Widget
3. Creating Your First Playbook

FIGURE 15.1   Example of a Drift chatbot responding to a customer support question.

no-brainer. Not only does it allow for a smoother transition for customers, as they don't have to adapt to a new customer communication system, but it contributes to a stronger, more cohesive brand experience overall.

Remember: Your company's brand isn't its logo or its mascot or its mission statement. Instead, your brand is a reflection of the experiences people have with your company. And every single interaction contributes to how your brand is perceived. So while the task of brand building is often assigned to marketing teams or design teams, it's important to recognize that top-of-the-funnel interactions aren't the only interactions shaping your brand. As CEO of the team collaboration platform Slack, Stewart Butterfield, wrote in an email to employees (which he later published on Medium), ". . . even the best slogans, ads, landing pages, PR campaigns, etc., will fall down if they are not supported by the experience people have when they hit our site, when they sign up for an account, when they first begin using the product, and when they start using it day in, day out."

The big takeaway here: Building a brand isn't about doing one thing well. It's about providing a stellar experience every step of the way for everyone you interact with—visitors, leads, and customers. By taking a conversational approach to supporting customers in conjunction with using conversational marketing and sales, you'll earn a reputation for being a company that truly cares about the experiences people are having when they visit your website, regardless of where those people happen to be in their customer journeys. *That's* how you build a brand that people love—one positive interaction at a time.

Staying Close to Your Customers (Through Continuous Feedback)

In addition to allowing you to provide a cohesive, real-time experience throughout every stage of a person's customer journey, adopting a conversational approach after the sale allows you to easily and painlessly gather customer feedback, which you can then use to refine the customer experience even further.

Customer feedback is like a battery that powers customer-driven companies. It has a positive side ("We love your product!") and a negative side ("Your product stinks!"), but you need both—the positive feedback and the negative feedback—in order to get a significant output. Remember: Your customers are the people who are using and (ideally) getting value from your product or service day in, day out, which means they know better than you do when it comes to how their experience could be better. Unfortunately, many companies have been either devaluing or outright ignoring the valuable feedback their customers have been providing. Instead of listening to customers and adapting to their evolving expectations, many of us have been relying on our own instincts and on ideas developed internally. We've been company-driven instead of customer-driven.

These days, in a world in which customers have all the power and where on-demand experiences have become the norm, a company-driven approach will no longer cut it. These days, in order to achieve hypergrowth, companies— SaaS companies in particular—need to be able to update their product regularly and rapidly and make improvements to their processes based on the customer feedback they gather through real-time conversations.

Building a Feedback Loop

As an entrepreneur, I've been obsessed with customer feedback loops since I built my very first website as a college student. Back then, in the heyday of web browsers like Mosaic and, later, Netscape, it was common to put your email address in the footer of your website, so that's exactly what I did. And then, one day, it happened—a monumental event. Someone sent me this message:

"Hey man, I really like your website. It's really cool."

Just like that, I had experienced my first customer feedback loop (see Figure 15.2). With every company I've

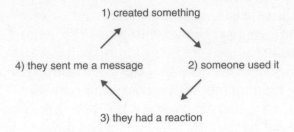

FIGURE 15.2 Diagram of a basic customer feedback loop.

founded and every team I've run since then, gathering customer feedback and having a real-time pulse on how customers feel about our products have been crucial to how we've operated.

Starting in 2009, while I was CEO at Performable, I sort of stumbled into this customer-driven approach to supporting customers, wherein our engineers would talk directly to our customers and fix bugs and make other updates, on the fly, based on their real-time feedback. I say "stumbled into" because the reason our engineers were doing support in the first place was that we were a small, scrappy startup made up mostly of engineers. We didn't have a dedicated customer support team yet. So it was all hands on deck. Everyone took a shift supporting customers.

We soon discovered that by allowing these one-to-one support conversations to happen between our engineers (the people who were working on our product day in, day out) and our customers (the people who were using our product day in, day out) we were able to resolve product issues much, much more quickly. In fact, I still know former customers from back then who remember being able to message us with an issue and within minutes we'd be able to tell them, "Hit refresh," and the issue would be resolved. These one-to-one conversations also allowed us to glean insights into how we could make our overall product more aligned with the problems our customers needed help solving and the metrics they needed help moving.

When Performable was acquired by HubSpot in 2011 and I became HubSpot's chief product officer, I brought my conversational, customer-driven approach to supporting customers with me and began refining it. Then, when I launched Drift in 2014, I made sure being conversational and customer-driven was baked into how we operated from the very start. And now we're helping other companies adopt the same approach.

Today, business leaders around the world are seeing the value in having one-to-one conversations with their customers, including Peter Reinhardt, co-founder and CEO of the customer data platform company Segment. As Reinhardt wrote on his personal blog, when trying to find product/market fit for some of his product ideas (one of which would eventually become Segment), he was originally hesitant to pursue customer conversations as a resource. "As engineers who had never done this before, talking to people didn't seem like real work. Real work was coding," he wrote. "But in reality, 20 hours of great interviews probably would've saved us an accrued 18 months of building useless stuff."

Ultimately, talking to people one-on-one is the best way to collect customer feedback and identify customer problems. In addition to using this feedback to improve your product (or to fine-tune a product idea), you can use it to improve the experience customers have on your website. For the CMO of the data science software company RapidMiner, Tom Wentworth (whom I mentioned way back in Chapter Four), being able to improve the on-site experience for customers is crucial, as one of RapidMiner's most important company goals is to keep their customers happy and engaged. In order to achieve this goal at scale, Tom uses a chatbot to ask customers on the RapidMiner website, "Why are you here?"

"So by asking that simple question I start to figure out patterns around things that maybe my website's not doing today that it should be," Tom told the Drift marketing team. "So these conversations have actually spurred us to rethink: What's the structure of our website? What's the information that we should be surfacing more easily because customers have these questions and we're not answering them?"

After implementing a conversational strategy on his website, Tom found that customers who engaged in real-time conversations ended up being 30% more likely to remain monthly active users of RapidMiner and also had a 20% higher Net Promoter Score (NPS), which is an indication of how satisfied customers are with your product and how loyal they are to your company.

The main takeaway here: Listening to (and acting on) the feedback you receive from customers is crucial to keeping your product—as well as the overall customer experience you're providing—aligned with the expectations of your customers. That being said, not all business leaders believe that their customers know best.

What About That Famous Henry Ford Quote?

"If I had asked people what they wanted, they would have said faster horses."

The above quote, often attributed to Henry Ford, seems to cast doubt on the notion that customer feedback is essential to the success of your product and/or business. After all, in 1908, when the Ford Motor Company debuted the Model T—the first mass-market automobile—it took the world by storm. And as the quote implies, this transportation breakthrough wasn't necessarily something people were asking for. Arguably, it was Ford's own visionary thinking that led to the Model T's success.

But here's the part of the story most people aren't usually as familiar with: By the 1920s, customer expectations had shifted. Car buyers weren't just interested in buying any old car anymore; they wanted cars that suited their individual lifestyles. That's exactly how Ford's competitors, most notably General Motors, began to eat away at the Model T's market share: by listening to customer feedback and giving customers what they were asking for.

Ford, meanwhile, doubled-down on his one-size-fits-all Model T. He refused to abandon his original vision. In 1921, the Ford Motor Company was selling 60% of the cars it was manufacturing. By 1927, that figure had dropped to 15%.

Perhaps not surprisingly, 1927 was also the year that Ford finally decided to retire the Model T and replace it with something more modern, the Model A. But by then, the damage had already been done.

As the author and entrepreneur Patrick Vlaskovits wrote in the *Harvard Business Review*, it's unclear whether Henry Ford actually uttered the quote, "If I had asked people what they wanted, they would have said faster horses," in his lifetime. However, it is clear to Vlaskovits that Ford "most certainly did think along those lines," and that "his tone-deafness to customers' needs (explicit or implicit), had a very costly and negative impact on the Ford Motor Company's investors, employees, and customers."

Ultimately, Ford's belief that customers were incapable of communicating what they were looking for in a product was proven to be inaccurate, and Ford's company ended up suffering as a result. As Vlaskovits so elegantly concluded in his article about Ford's famous quote: "It was clear what people wanted, and it wasn't faster horses. It was better cars, with better financing options."

What to Do with Customer Feedback Once You Collect It

Throughout this chapter, we've been exploring the importance of listening to customers and how you can use customer feedback in order to make continual improvements to your product and processes. In theory this sounds extremely straightforward, but I often see companies get tripped up when it comes to taking the customer feedback they've gathered, prioritizing it, and making it actionable. This was definitely something we struggled with early on at Drift. With messaging and chatbots rolled out across our website, allowing us to have conversations around the clock, we were gathering more customer feedback than we knew what to do with (which wasn't a terrible problem to have).

To solve that problem, we developed the Spotlight Framework (see Table 15.1), which allows us to quickly and easily categorize the type of feedback we're hearing so we can then take the appropriate next steps.

The key to using the framework is to focus on the opening words and phrases of what your customers are telling you. Chances are, you'll be able to diagnose the type of issues you're dealing with based solely on how customers structure their feedback.

For years, we've been focused on the wrong part of the feedback we've been hearing from customers. Instead of honing in on the broader, underlying issue someone's feedback has been pointing to, we've tended to focus on the subject of the feedback. In doing so, we've been failing to take the right next steps.

For example, if we keep hearing the question, "How do I turn on this feature?" over and over, we might be tempted to think, "Hey, this feature must be really popular. All of our customers keep asking about it." But when you use the Spotlight Framework, you can see right away that the underlying issue here is a user experience issue—the customer knows something is possible, he or she just can't figure out how to do it inside of your product. That's why the questions keep coming in. That should send a signal to your product team that they may need to make an update.

TABLE 15.1 The Spotlight Framework for processing customer feedback.

User Experience Issue	Product Marketing Issue	Positioning Issue
"How do I . . ."	"Can you/I . . ."	"I'm probably not your target customer . . ."
"What happens when . . ."	"How do you compare to . . ."	"I'm sure I'm wrong but I thought . . ."
"I tried to . . ."	"How are you different than . . ."	
	"Why should I use you for/to . . ."	

Alternatively, if a customer asks a question like, "Can you integrate with this platform?" the framework shows you that this is a product marketing issue—the customer isn't sure whether something is possible or not, which sends a signal to your product marketing team that they may need to mention integrations more prominently on your website.

Finally, we have positioning issues. Usually, you can diagnose these issues based on how nice the people are in giving their feedback. For example, if a person comes to your website and says something that starts with "I'm probably not your target customer, but . . . ," and it turns out that person *is* actually a target customer, that's a sign that your positioning is off—people aren't sure whether they're a good fit for your product even when they are. Another sign you might have a positioning issue is if a customer says something that starts with, "I'm sure I'm wrong about this, but I thought . . . ," and it turns out his or her assumption is correct. That lack of clarity is a sign that you may need to revisit how you're positioning your product to the world.

By organizing your customer feedback into these three categories—user experience issues, product marketing issues, and positioning issues—you'll more easily be able to determine the next course of action you need to take based on that feedback. Best of all, if you're using a conversational marketing and sales platform, you can "tag" the real-time conversations you're having with these customers when these specific issues arise. That way everyone on your team will be able to better understand which types of issues customers are experiencing most frequently.

Prioritizing Customer Feedback

While you can use the Spotlight Framework to organize customer feedback and to figure out the next step that needs to be taken to make that feedback actionable, there's still a matter of prioritization. When you're having dozens, hundreds, or thousands of conversations with customers every day, figuring out which feedback to act on immediately, which feedback to sit on, and which feedback to ignore can be challenging. This is especially the case for SaaS companies—like Drift—that offer free products in addition to paid plans because it means we're hearing feedback—including requests for new product features—from two different categories of people: free users and paying customers.

The secret to prioritizing feedback in these tricky situations is to not only distinguish between who you're talking to—a free user or a customer—but also to monitor the frequency with which you're hearing a particular question, concern, or feature request being voiced.

Think of it as a spectrum: At one extreme, you have tons of paying customers all requesting that you add the same new feature to your product, and these requests are becoming more and more frequent. In these instances, you should take action to implement that new feature as quickly as possible. Clearly, if a bunch of customers—the people using your product day in, day out—are telling you about a hole they've detected in what you're offering, resolving that should become a top priority.

At the other extreme, you have a feature request coming from a free user, and it's the first time you've ever heard that particular request from anyone. In such an instance, it's not a priority to make a change. As a customer support rep, what you should do instead is ask more questions and see whether you can learn more.

For a single *paying* customer who requests a one-off new feature, however, you should make a note of the request (and/ or tag the conversation in your conversational marketing and sales platform) and revisit it later. While it may not be a top priority today, it could become eventually. You can take the same course of action when dealing with a feature request that multiple free users (but not paying customers) have been requesting. While it doesn't necessarily require immediate action, it's something you'll definitely want to keep an eye on.

Ultimately, you should always weigh the opinions and concerns of your paying customers more heavily compared with those of your free users. Whereas the former group already understands the value your company can provide, the latter group is still testing the waters and figuring out whether you'd be a good fit. If you look back at the Spotlight Framework, feedback from free users tends to fall into the "product marketing issue" category. That's because free users are still trying to understand what your product can do (hence, you hear questions that start with, "Can I . . . "). Feedback from paying customers, on the other hand, tends to fall into the "user experience issue" category. That's because most customers already know what your product can do, so instead they want to learn how they can squeeze even more value out of your product by making things faster or easier (hence, you hear questions that start with, "How do I . . .").

Inevitably, of course, you are going to have to say "no" (at least temporarily) to a feature request that comes from a customer. In those instances, it's important to remember that even though you have to say "no" to the request, you don't have to end the conversation with a "no." Instead, you can ask questions and treat every conversation you have with a customer as an opportunity to learn.

Chapter 16

A Conversational Approach to Customer Success

In the previous chapter, we looked at having conversations with customers primarily as a reactive activity. We explored, from a customer support perspective, how teams can use conversations in order to listen to customer concerns (and feature requests) as soon as customers voice them. However, as many of you already know, those aren't the only types of conversations you should be having with customers after the sale. Today, in addition to having a customer support team that reacts to customer issues as they arise, you should have a customer success team that proactively engages with customers and helps them become as successful with your product as possible. Not only will it result in a better customer experience, but it will help improve your business's bottom line.

Depending on the industry you're in (and the specific data you look at), the cost of acquiring a new customer is anywhere from five to 25 times more expensive than the cost of retaining an existing customer, according to *Harvard Business Review* contributing editor Amy Gallo. "It makes sense: you don't have to spend time and resources going out and finding a new client—you just have to keep the one you have happy," Gallo wrote in a 2014 article.

Meanwhile, the probability of upselling an existing customer (which we'll learn more about later in this chapter) and getting that customer to buy from you again is around 60 to 70%, while the probability of getting a prospect to buy from you for the first time is only around 5% to 20%, according to the book *Marketing Metrics* (Farris, Bendle, Pfeifer, and Reibstein, 2011).

The takeaway here: It's not enough to be reacting to your customers. In order for your business to thrive, you need your customers to thrive. Taking a proactive approach to ensuring your customers are happy and successful isn't just the right thing to do from a customer experience perspective, it's the smart thing to do from a revenue perspective. It all starts as soon as a customer dives into your product for the first time and begins learning the ropes.

Overhauling the Traditional Approach to Onboarding

At Drift, our customer success managers schedule kickoff calls with new customers as early as possible. They use these calls to talk about goals and metrics and to help customers set milestones so they can see the progress they're making.

Of course, the kickoff call is a pretty standard part of the customer onboarding process, especially for SaaS companies, and as long as your customers find them valuable, there's no reason to stop doing them. But, in order to make those conversations more focused and relevant, you can set up chatbots that target new customers on your website and/or inside of your app to prep new customers for those kickoff calls. You can also have chatbots schedule kickoff calls for you (just as Sales uses them to schedule demos and meetings). It's the same conversational experience you've been learning about throughout the book, only now you're applying it to your onboarding. For new customers, it means they don't have to play phone or email tag in order to set up a time to talk. Instead, they can get responses and schedule meetings in real time.

Building an Onboarding Bot

If you've read Chapter Ten, you already understand how to set up a simple lead qualification chatbot. The good news: Setting up a chatbot to assist your customer success team with new customer onboarding will adhere to the same rules and mechanics we've already learned about. The only difference is that now the objective of your chatbot conversations has changed, which means you'll need to update your questions and responses in order to reflect that. Since your new customers (we hope) already understand the value of your product, at this stage you no longer need to use chatbots to figure out whether someone is a good fit to buy. Instead, you can use chatbots to figure out how to bring someone up and running with your product as quickly as possible, based on that customer's specific needs.

At Drift, we built a chatbot that appears to new customers when they open our app for the first time. After welcoming customers to the Drift family, we have the chatbot ask the new customer a few quick questions, the answers to which help our customer success managers double-check a few key pieces of information ahead of the kickoff call. Specifically, we have our new customer onboarding chatbot ask the following four questions:

1. What website are you looking to use Drift on?
2. What's your primary goal for using Drift?
3. Do you have any tools you're looking to integrate?
4. Now a fun one. What's your t-shirt size?

Yes, that fourth question is crucial. (And yes, so is that t-shirt emoji we include at the end of it.) After the chatbot takes a new customer's t-shirt size, our customer success team sends a t-shirt, along with some other Drift swag, out to that customer the same day. At the end of the conversation, the chatbot prompts the new customer to set up an onboarding call and gives him or her access to a customer success manager's calendar so he or she can book a day and time that works best.

Remember: The goal of using chatbots here isn't to remove human customer success managers from the onboarding experience; it's to help those customer success managers enter conversations at the right times, armed with tons of context.

Introducing Customers to Different Parts of Your Product

In addition to building a chatbot that can prep new customers for their onboarding calls, you can also build chatbots that proactively introduce new customers to the different parts of your product.

For example, at Drift, we built a chatbot that pops up for our customers the first time they navigate to the settings menu of our app (see Figure 16.1). The chatbot asks whether a customer needs help and provides a checklist of the different tasks it can help with.

Whether your custom success managers are currently offline or you have customers who simply prefer doing everything themselves, chatbots give the customers the ability to receive structured product guidance 24 hours a day, and those conversations can happen directly inside of your product. For SaaS companies, that's another key benefit of adopting messaging and chatbots: In addition to having Marketing and Sales use them to target specific leads (and types of leads) on your website, your customer success managers can use them to target specific customers (and types of customers) inside of your app. Behind the scenes, inside of your conversational marketing and sales platform, the only thing that changes—apart from what you're saying, of course—is how you target your conversations.

In addition to targeting people based on firmographic data and the behaviors they've displayed on your website, once those people close into customers and log into your product, you can start targeting them based on their product usage. That way, as a customer success team, you can make sure you're always reaching out at the right times with the right messages. For example, if you notice that customers are spending lots of time on the billing page inside of your

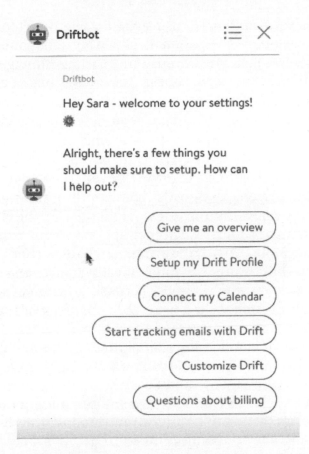

FIGURE 16.1   Example of a chatbot designed to help new customers navigate the settings menu inside the Drift app.

app, you could create a chatbot specifically for that page that asks customers what they're stuck on and then have the bot offer some solutions.

Opening a Fast Lane to Your Customer Success Managers

According to a 2016 study from Forrester, 73% of customers believe that the most important element of good customer service is respecting a person's time. And that's exactly why adopting a conversational approach to customer success will allow you to deliver a superior customer experience: As a customer success manager, you'll be able to open a fast lane for your paying customers and reduce (or completely eliminate) the time they might usually have spent waiting to get in touch with you.

With messaging, a single customer success manager can engage in multiple conversations, helping multiple customers simultaneously instead of just one at a time. And remember back in Chapter Eleven, when I explained how sales teams can use intelligent routing to ensure that leads always are routed to the right sales reps based on their ownership rules? Customer success teams can do the same thing, ensuring that during messaging conversations, customers will always be automatically routed to customer success managers who already understand how those customers are using your product and what their specific goals are. That way, your customer success managers will be able to focus all of their time and energy on actually helping customers and solving problems (and not on trying to bring other people at your company up to speed).

Of course, as I've already mentioned, human customer success managers can't stay online around the clock. At some point, they're going to need to eat and sleep and go on vacation. And that's where chatbots come in. In addition to using them as onboarding tools, customer success teams can use chatbots the same way sales reps do—as backup. For example, if a customer asks a question via messaging while inside of your app, but everyone on your team is offline, you can have a chatbot step in and provide answers to those questions by linking to relevant help docs and other content.

Compared to emailing back and forth, having a real-time conversation, whether it's with a human or a chatbot, allows customers to find answers to their questions more quickly. And that's exactly why the customer loyalty platform company Swipii decided to adopt a conversational approach to customer success. As Swipii's head of marketing, Robert Gillespie, told the Drift marketing team: "We needed something that we didn't need to mess about [with]. Just someplace users could go into very quickly, get their answer, or if not, jump into a conversation with us in real time." That, right there, is the perfect description of the fast lane your customer success team can create for your customers using messaging and chatbots. Best of all, you can create this customer success fast lane without having to make any drastic changes to your existing setup or software stack. As Robert explained, "It was literally a plug and play solution for us."

Using Real-Time Conversations in the Battle Against Churn

Ultimately, setting up a customer success fast lane with messaging and chatbots will allow you to provide a frictionless, pain-free way for customers to get in touch with you and to find the answers and information they're looking for. For customer success teams (SaaS customer success teams in particular), that's really good news. Because, as it turns out, delivering that type of customer experience is crucial to helping you retain customers and reduce your company's churn rate.

For those unfamiliar with the term, "churn" refers to the percentage of a company's customers who quit a product or service in a given period of time. Research from CEB shows that if a company subjects a customer to a "high effort experience," where a customer has difficulty finding help or has to repeat himself or herself several times, that customer will be more likely to churn. In fact, CEB found that 96% of customers would become disloyal or leave a company after being subjected to a high effort experience. Meanwhile, research conducted by Bain & Company's Frederick Reichheld— creator of the Net Promoter Score (NPS)—shows that a 5% increase in a company's customer retention rates will lead to an increase in profits of between 25% and 95%. The takeaway here: If you make things easy for your customers, not only will they be more likely to stick around, but they'll help your bottom line.

By using messaging and chatbots to streamline how you manage customer communication and to provide round-the-clock, real-time service, you can ensure that you never subject customers to high effort experiences. And while setting up fast lanes both on your website and inside of your app will already put you on the right track toward keeping customer churn below 5% (which is an informal but widely known SaaS benchmark for where your churn rate should be), you can also take a more proactive approach. In addition to using messaging and chatbots to start conversations with customers when they're already on your site or in your product, you can use email to start conversations with customers when they're not around.

The Four Customer Emails You Should Start Sending Today

When a customer is at risk of churning, you can't sit around and wait for that customer to start a conversation with you on your website or inside your app. After all, if this is someone who has stopped using your product, you're never going to reach him or her with an in-app message. In these instances, before you have to escalate to making a phone call, email is your best option.

Just as with messaging, you can target emails to customers based on the behaviors they display (or don't display) inside of your product. That way, you can use email to help nudge customers in the right direction, or to nudge them back into your product so they can start deriving value from it.

While email isn't everyone's preferred communication channel these days, it can still be useful—especially when you use it as a tool for rekindling customer conversations. As you saw in Chapter Six, and again in Chapter Thirteen, by including links in your emails that trigger conversations (with humans, if they're available, and with chatbots, if not), you'll be able to transform email into a real-time customer communication channel that you can use to proactively battle churn.

Here are four emails you can start with. You can use them (and personalize them) as part of automated sequences or send them one-to-one.

1. **The welcome email.** Yes, this one's pretty standard, but I didn't want to skip over it. Even when you're using messaging to welcome new customers on your website and inside of your app, you should send out a welcome email as part of new customer onboarding. Just make sure that in addition to welcoming new customers aboard, you use that email to ask customers a question, even if it's a simple, "Why did you decide to buy?" Remember: The goal of email shouldn't be to blast out a one-sided message, but to engage someone in conversation.

2. **The three-days-later email.** The number of days here is arbitrary. Whether it's two days, three days, or four days after you send your welcome email, you can send out a follow-up email that provides tips for getting started with (and getting the most value out of) your product. While some customers will explore every nook and cranny of your product and end up learning a lot on their own (with the help of some chatbots you've set up), other customers require more hands-on attention. It's important to make sure those customers learn how to get things up and running quickly so they can start seeing results as quickly as possible (and not become disengaged).

3. **The inactive customer check-in email.** For customers who go a week or so without using your product, you may want to send an email that asks whether there's something wrong or something your company could be doing better. Again, the precise number of days you wait before sending this email is up to you, but the underlying goal is the same: to reach out to customers at the very first indication that they've become disengaged with your product. That way, you can identify where those customers are struggling and help them get back on track before they decide to churn.

4. **The 30-day renewal notice email.** This one's a bit more administrative in its scope, but it's still an email that can literally help you prevent churn. Here's the setup: A customer's credit card has expired, but his or her subscription is set to renew. What do you do? By sending an email 30 days or so before a customer's subscription renews, you can help ensure that you don't lose customers to churn as a result of their payment

information being out of date. What's more, you can use these renewal notice emails to start conversations around (and to gauge interest in) customers upgrading to higher tiers of your product and/or purchasing additional functionality.

In the final section of this chapter, we're going to explore in more detail how customer success managers can use a conversational approach not only to serve customers better and reduce churn but also to sell customers on other product plans and features.

Conversational Upselling 101

Many businesspeople tend to think about increasing revenue as a job for their marketing and sales teams. The reality is that you're much more likely to generate new revenue from your existing customers than you are from new customers. As SaaS entrepreneur and investor Jason Lemkin said at the 2015 Gainsight Pulse conference: "Customer success is where 90% of the revenue is."

In addition to existing customers being a huge—and in many cases, untapped—source of revenue, selling to your existing customers is much more cost-effective compared to selling to new customers. According to research from David Skok's for *Entrepreneur*'s blog, the cost of acquiring $1 from a new customer is 68% more expensive than the cost of upselling existing customers.

The takeaway here: If you're not actively upselling (or cross-selling) your customers, you're missing out. And to clarify, by upselling and cross-selling, I don't mean bombarding customers with messages telling them that they need to start paying more. Instead, the goal is to help them along their customer journey and to introduce higher tiered plans (upselling) or supplemental tools and features (cross-selling) as part of an ongoing customer conversation. (Note: For the sake of convenience, moving forward I'm going to use the umbrella term "upselling" to refer to both concepts.)

Unlike churn, which is an indication of how good (or bad) you are at persuading customers to stick around, the amount of revenue you generate through upselling is an indication of how good you are at getting customers to grow with your product. By adopting a conversational approach to customer success, and having ongoing conversations with customers, you can identify upsell opportunities and take proactive steps toward persuading customers to upgrade.

New Feature Announcements

In Chapter Fifteen, we explored how companies can use customer feedback in order to decide what new features they should add to their products. But once your product team designs those features and your engineering team builds them and launches them, that's not the end of the story: You need to let your customers know about the changes. Sending an email is one option, but for SaaS companies, a better option is to have your new feature announcement pop up directly inside of your app. In addition to targeting your messages to specific segments of customers (based on their product behavior, for example), you can build a chatbot that asks qualifying questions—just the way you learned how to do in Chapter Ten—to ensure that customers are a good fit for the new feature you're introducing.

Targeted In-App Messages

Of course, you can use in-app messages for more than just making new feature announcements. You can use them to highlight any product feature or functionality that you think a specific customer (or segment of customers) could benefit from adopting or to highlight a product plan that you think a specific customer (or segment of customers) should upgrade to.

In the SaaS world, it's common for companies to have different tiers of product plans, some of which are aimed at the enterprise and come with all the bells and whistles, while others are aimed at individual users and offer a more stripped-down set of features. With in-app messages, customer success managers can easily differentiate among the different types of customers they're engaging with and set up personalized messages (and chatbots) that can target customers at specific moments in their customer journeys. For example, you could create an in-app message that only pops up for your business-tier customers who are trying to explore a part of your product that's only included in your enterprise plan. The welcome message could ask whether those customers wanted to learn more about that specific feature, and—if the answer was yes—those customers could be routed accordingly (either directly to a customer success manager for a real-time conversation, to a qualifying chatbot, or to a customer success manager's calendar).

"At Capacity" Warning Messages

For many SaaS companies, their product pricing hinges on how much data or storage their customers are using or how many contacts those customers are storing in contacts databases. In cases like these, customer success teams can use in-app messages in order to call out when customers are about to reach their limits. For example, if you notice that a customer will soon use up all of the storage that came with his or her current product plan, you can send an in-app message (and/or an email) to warn that customer ahead of time and to help that customer figure out the product plan that will be the best fit for him or her moving forward.

One final takeaway for bringing a conversational upselling strategy to life: Don't overdo it.

While your existing customers are an incredibly valuable source of knowledge as well as revenue, make sure you give them room to breathe. Remember: These are people who have already discovered the value of your product and have decided it's worth their money. Instead of hitting them over the head with upsell opportunities, you should serve as a personal guide and take a conversational approach to helping your customers discover the value of the features or functionality they're still missing out on.

Chapter 17

Measuring Conversational Marketing and Sales Performance

O ne of our core values at Drift is "always be learning." But this isn't just some empty phrase we hang on the wall, it's something we use in our hiring process—we actively seek out employees who have voracious appetites for knowledge. "Always be learning" also serves as the foundation for our podcast, Seeking Wisdom, which, as the name implies, is a show dedicated to the pursuit of learning and uncovering new insights so we can improve both personally and professionally.

Of course, as you saw back in Chapter Fifteen, we also apply our "always be learning" philosophy to our customers by using conversations to create continuous feedback loops. Ultimately, our customers are the ones who dictate what their experience feels like, as we're able to listen to their feedback and continuously make improvements. As a result, we'll always be able to adapt to their evolving needs and expectations.

In a perfect world, this type of knowledge—which you're able to gain via having real-time conversations with website visitors, leads, and customers—would be enough to justify investing in a conversational approach. But look, I get it. As a five-time founder and two-time CEO, I understand that from a business perspective, marketing and sales teams (as well as customer support and success teams) need to be able to tie everything they do back to revenue. As we explored in Chapter Five, revenue is the glue that holds marketing and sales teams together. By adopting a conversational approach and aligning Marketing and Sales around the shared goal of driving revenue, you'll finally be able to put an end to the bickering—no more arguing over leads.

When you're capturing, qualifying, and connecting with customers via messaging, it's easy to go back and see how conversations started, as well as how they ended. (In a meeting? In a sale?) By analyzing these different outcomes, you'll be able to tie all of the conversations you're having back to actual revenue. That way, everyone at your business, including your board members and investors, will be able to see the value of adopting a conversational approach. What's more, by measuring the performance of your conversational marketing and sales efforts, you'll be able to identify which pieces of your strategy are working the best—and generating the most revenue—and which pieces need updating.

The bottom line: To ensure you're achieving your growth goals, you need to monitor your growth. And that means paying regular attention to certain metrics and grading your day-to-day performance. Keep reading to learn about the conversational marketing and sales metrics you should be focusing on.

Sales Meetings Booked

Historically, booking sales meetings (and product demos) has been a pain. With all the email back-and-forths and games of phone tag, sales reps wasted a ton of their time scheduling when they should have been selling. Today, there are no excuses. After setting up messaging and lead qualification chatbots, marketing teams will be able to book meetings for sales reps 24 hours a day, seven days a week.

By looking at how many meetings you're booking on a daily, weekly, and monthly basis, and then seeing how many of those meetings convert to closed deals, you'll be able to develop a good baseline of how many meetings you need to book in order to hit your sales goals. While the number of leads you were generating used to be the "magic number" in marketing, the reality is that capturing someone's contact information is meaningless unless it leads to an actual conversation. That's why meetings are a better metric to measure.

At TrainedUp, a company I first mentioned back in Chapter Eleven, they pay specific attention to how many meetings (or in their case, product demos) their chatbots are able to book for them. And what they've found is that 15% of chatbot-only conversations—conversations during which chatbots do all the talking on behalf of your business—end up converting into demos. And 40% of those demos result in closed deals. (The company also knows that, on average, those customers tend to close within a month of their demos.)

In addition to monitoring *how many* sales meetings you're booking, it's important to monitor *who* you're having those meetings with. That's why your sales team should keep a real-time list of all of the upcoming meetings they have in a given week (see Figure 17.1). In addition to allowing for increased transparency at your company, keeping this type of list will give you a more detailed understanding of what deals are coming down the pipe (and when), which in turn will allow you to forecast deals with greater precision.

The best part: If you're using a conversational marketing and sales platform, there's no manual labor required in order to build and maintain a list like this. Once your sales reps have connected their calendars, a conversational marketing and sales platform can do all of the work for you and update the list automatically as sales meetings start pouring in.

Opportunities Added

Ideally, at the end of a sales meeting, a sales rep will either (a) close a deal—definitely a best-case scenario, or (b) at least confirm that a lead is serious about buying

Who's Booking Meetings with Us?
This week so far

BOOKED WITH	COMPANY	NAME	TITLE
James Pidgeon	SalesRabbit	Chelsea Ward	Director of Inside Sal(
Ally Brez	Segment	Jane Meyer	VP of Marketing
Danielle Tocci	Rapidminer	Sara Ortega	Director of Content
Brendan McManus	Leadpages	Pete Read	VP of Sales
Alex Hanbury	ThriveHive	Andy Scott	Principal

FIGURE 17.1 Mockup of a list that shows, in real time, who's booking meetings with your sales reps.

and that there's actual money on the table. This latter category, which sits between "qualified lead" and "customer" at the bottom of your sales funnel, is known as an "opportunity."

Of course, all businesses define the difference between leads and qualified leads and opportunities differently, but in general, you can think about it like this: A qualified lead can be someone who's only engaged with a chatbot. An opportunity, on the other hand, is someone who has engaged with a (human) sales rep and that sales rep has identified that person as being not only a good fit for the product but also as being a real revenue opportunity for the business.

As I mentioned way back in Chapter One, the open-source database program company MongoDB was able to grow opportunities by 170% after switching to a conversational approach. Specifically, they used targeted messaging and chatbots in order to filter out the "noise" on their website, only allowing qualified leads to schedule meetings with their sales reps. So no wonder MongoDB was able to increase opportunities—their sales reps were being handed the best possible leads to engage with.

Pipeline Influenced

In addition to keeping an eye on the number (and percentage) of opportunities you're creating via real-time conversations, you can monitor the total dollar amount associated with those opportunities—commonly known as "pipeline."

Depending on your pricing, selling one higher-tier plan can bring in the revenue equivalent of selling five or ten lower-tier plans. The point being: If you want to understand how real-time conversations are affecting your bottom line, you need to look at how much of your sales pipeline conversations are influencing it. And that's exactly what CMO Tom Wentworth does over at RapidMiner. As I mentioned in Chapter Four, within months of adopting conversational marketing and sales, RapidMiner saw conversations influence 25% of all of their open sales pipeline, which was worth more than $1 million.

Closed/Won

How much of your sales pipeline ends up turning into actual revenue? That's closed/won: It's the total dollar amount associated with opportunities who ink deals and become paying customers.

On its own, closed/won is an essential metric, as it shows you how much revenue you're generating with conversational marketing and sales. But you can make it even more powerful by monitoring it alongside other metrics related to revenue, such as pipeline influenced and opportunities (see Figure 17.2). That way, you'll be able to see the progression of leads as they move through the bottom of your funnel.

Conversation Metrics

Yes, I've already established that revenue is the "one metric to rule them all" when it comes to measuring conversational marketing and sales performance. But when you zoom

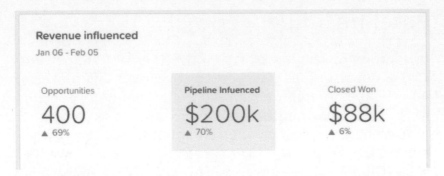

FIGURE 17.2 Mockup of a conversational sales reporting dashboard displaying three key metrics: opportunities, pipeline, and closed/won.

in and try to understand how you can do a better job of generating revenue via real-time conversations, it makes sense to learn everything you can about the conversations you're having—from how many new conversations are being started, to when those conversations are happening, to where those conversations are happening, to who at your company is participating in those conversations. These are all metrics you can monitor inside of a conversational marketing and sales platform. Now let's take a close look.

New Conversations

Every sale starts with a conversation. That's why it's a good idea to track how many new conversations you're having on your website. By comparing how many conversations you're starting day-to-day, week-to-week, and month-to-month (see Figure 17.3), you'll be able to measure the pulse of your conversational strategy and make adjustments accordingly. For example, if you notice a drop in new conversations, that might be a sign that you need to rethink your targeting and/ or update the copy you're using for your welcome messages and chatbot scripts.

The business analytics company Databox was able to increase new conversations by 113% after reworking their chatbot script. As Databox's director of marketing, John Bonini, explained in a blog post on the Databox blog, "While we were seeing results, we were curious if we could 10x the

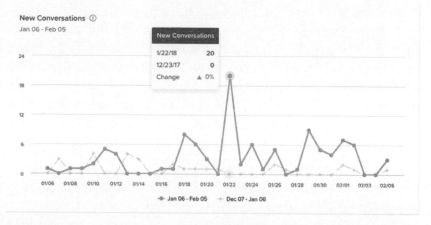

FIGURE 17.3 Mockup of a month-to-month comparison of how many new conversations are being started on a website.

engagement by going more open-ended and conversational." So Bonini dug into the conversation data (stored in his conversational marketing and sales platform) and began to hone in on the most common reasons people were coming to the Databox website. As he explained, "By analyzing our conversations over the last six months, we learned that most everyone visiting our homepage (or pricing page) either wanted to (1) see a demo of the product, (2) learn more about pricing, or (3) simply talk to a real person." Armed with these new insights, Bonini rewrote his chatbot script to put these three options front and center (see Figure 17.4).

One last thing to keep in mind here: When measuring new conversations, you can filter according to who's

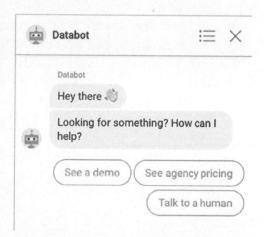

FIGURE 17.4 After analyzing six months' worth of conversations, Databox updated their chatbot script—increasing new conversations by 113%.

doing the talking—a human, a chatbot, or a chatbot-assisted human (where both a human and a chatbot participate in a conversation). That way, you'll be able to get a more granular understanding of how conversations are being distributed between humans and bots. As I mentioned in Chapter Three, at Drift we've seen that around 50% of new conversations are being managed by chatbots only, 40% are being managed by a mix of chatbots and humans, and only 10% are being managed by humans only.

New Conversations by Time of Day

In addition to looking at the volume of conversations you're having on your website, you can learn a lot from looking at *when* those conversations are happening. At Drift, we have a heatmap in our reporting dashboard that shows which times of the day are the most popular for new conversations (see Figure 17.5). The darker colors on the heatmap indicate that more conversations are happening in a given hour, while the lighter colors indicate that fewer conversations are happening.

Monitoring this data can help you get a better sense of when your website's busiest times are and, in turn, you can use the insights you gather to inform how you schedule messaging shifts. For example, it's a good idea to have human employees online during times when, historically, conversation volume has peaked. But during times when conversation volume has historically been low, you may choose to have chatbots be responsible for those shifts instead. The broader takeaway is that instead of arbitrarily scheduling online and offline hours for your team, you can look at new conversations by time of day in order to create a more informed scheduling system.

Conversation Locations

So far in this section, we've covered the importance of knowing *how many* conversations you're having on your website as well as knowing *when* you're having those conversations.

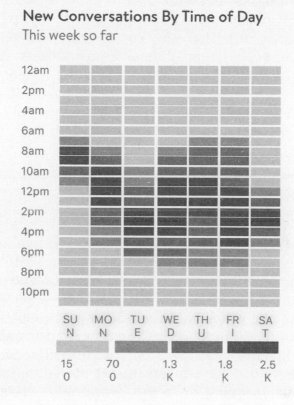

FIGURE 17.5 Mockup of a heatmap that shows what times of day new conversations are happening.

Now it's time to turn our attention to *where* those conversations are happening.

At Drift, we keep a real-time list of which pages of our website (and which sections of our app) are driving the most new conversations (see Figure 17.6). The list includes the specific number of conversations each page is driving, giving us even more insight into how our conversational marketing and sales efforts are paying off on those pages. But we don't look *only* at our top-performing pages. Since we track every single conversation that happens on our website (and in our product), we're also able to search for specific page URLs and look at conversation volume on a page-by-page basis. That, in turn,

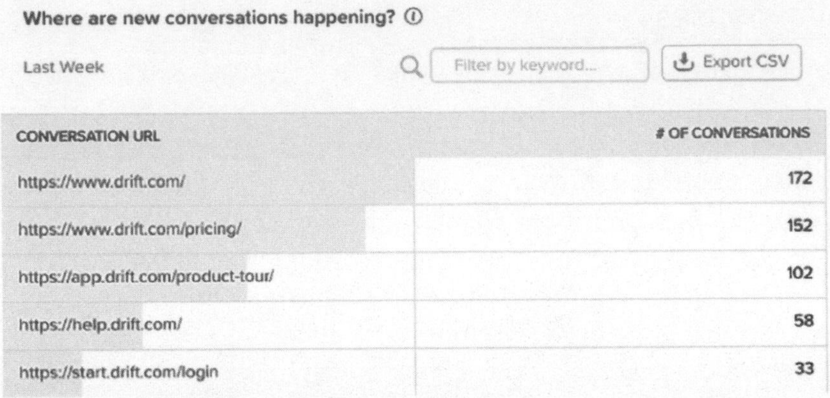

Where are new conversations happening? ⓘ

Last Week   🔍 Filter by keyword...   ⬇ Export CSV

CONVERSATION URL	# OF CONVERSATIONS
https://www.drift.com/	172
https://www.drift.com/pricing/	152
https://app.drift.com/product-tour/	102
https://help.drift.com/	58
https://start.drift.com/login	33

FIGURE 17.6 Mockup of how we monitor where conversations are happening on the Drift website.

allows us to identify low-performing pages so we can then figure out ways to improve them.

By knowing which pages on your website and/or which sections of your product are leading to the most (and fewest) conversations, you'll be able to better understand which pieces of your conversational marketing and sales strategy are working (and not working) and make the appropriate adjustments.

Team Performance Metrics

Conversational marketing and sales is a team sport. After all, every conversation that happens on your website contributes to the overall experience someone has with your company and with your brand. Every little interaction can contribute to a sale (or an upsell). And that means any employee who spends time talking to visitors, leads, and/or customers must be able to do a stellar job of communicating and providing the type of real-time service today's buyers have come to expect.

But how do you measure that? How do you know who, on your team, is doing a great job and who is falling behind? Keep reading to find out.

Responses

Here's one of the simplest ways to measure conversational marketing and sales productivity on your team: Look at who's replying to the most incoming conversations.

At Drift, we monitor—week over week and month over month—how many new conversations each of us is joining. That way, if conversation volume is low, we can potentially identify areas where people can step up and start engaging with more leads and customers.

Median Response Time

What is the median amount of time it takes your team—as well as individual employees on that team—to respond to visitors when they start conversations? That's median response time.

As I talked about in Chapter One, having a speedy response time is absolutely crucial when it comes to qualifying leads. Even if you wait just 5 minutes to respond to a new lead, your odds of ever connecting with that lead decrease by a magnitude of ten. Wait ten minutes, and there will be a 400% drop in your odds of qualifying that lead (according to research by InsideSales.com, published in the *Harvard Business Review*).

Of course, by using chatbots, you can guarantee that a lead always gets an instant response. But that's not what we're measuring here. If you're using chatbots, in order to calculate response time, you should look at how much time passes between the moment a person requests to chat with a human and the moment a human on your team is able to jump in and respond.

Median Conversation Length

After looking at who on your team is responding to the most incoming conversations, as well as who on your team is responding to conversations the fastest, you can look at who is having the longest (and shortest) conversations by calculating median conversation length. This metric indicates the median amount of time that passes between the moment an employee responds to a conversation and the moment an employee closes that conversation.

By monitoring median conversation length, you'll be able to identify any correlations that exist between how much time an employee spends talking with customers and how many meetings that employee is able to book, or how many deals he or she is able to close. For example, you might discover that sales reps with higher median conversation lengths end up bringing in more revenue because they're able to engage potential customers for longer and dig deeper into what problems those customers are trying to solve. Alternatively, for customer support reps, you might find that shorter median conversation lengths are superior, as they indicate that reps are able to provide concise answers and solve customer issues as quickly as possible.

Team Conversation Performance

In order to get a real-time snapshot of how your team is doing during any given week, I recommend setting up a conversation performance "scoreboard" that displays the three metrics we just discussed: responses to new conversations, median response time, and median conversations length (see Figure 17.7). While each metric can reveal its own insights, taken together they tell a more complete story about how your team—and each individual employee—is performing.

Ultimately, the goal of measuring these team perform metrics is to be able to hold yourself and your team accountable for providing the best customer experience possible. Remember: Every conversation matters. And every conversation presents an opportunity to learn.

Final Thought

I've always been obsessed with customer experience. I feel it every single day in my personal life: I want to buy from the businesses that make the process easy and enjoyable, and that treat me as if they care. But my obsession with the

Top Team Conversation Performance ⓘ

Last Week

NAME	Median Response Time	Median Conversation Length	# Of New Conversations ▼
Karla	2m 29s	20m 45s	40
Jeremy Lucas	1m 30s	10m 45	38
Tyra Earl	5m 45s	12m 56s	33
Sara Pion	3m 24s	4m 9s	25

FIGURE 17.7 Mockup of a team conversation performance "scoreboard."

customer experience doesn't just stem from it feeling nice to get great service as a consumer. It's because history tells us that the teams that get closest to their customers and provide the best customer experience possible always win.

Whether it's Amazon versus Borders, Netflix versus Blockbuster, or Uber and Lyft versus taxicabs, the companies that have been seeing the most extraordinary growth in recent years are the ones that have ignored age-old industry best practices in favor of developing a customer-driven approach. Instead of relying on what's already been done before, which would certainly make things easier *for them* (the companies), today's hypergrowth companies are putting the evolving needs and expectations of their customers ahead of everything else. They're laser-focused on delivering incredible experiences, even if that means being called crazy—or being told that their ideas could never scale.

During the early days of conversational marketing and sales, people told me all the time they didn't think having one-to-one conversations was scalable, or that providing real-time service was scalable. But instead of focusing on what the collective wisdom of the marketing and sales world was telling me, I listened to what customers were telling me.

If it weren't for the thousands of conversations I've had with customers over the years, this book you're reading right now wouldn't exist. All of the principles and best practices I've shared with you here have their roots in customer conversations. They all started as ideas (or really, the tiniest sparks of ideas) for solving customer problems that I gleaned through hearing feedback in one-to-one conversations. Regardless of whether it's a conversation you're having via messaging, email, or telephone, or in-person at a customer's office or in a coffee shop, the most important thing is that you're having a conversation. That's what marketing and sales has been missing.

I hope you now understand what steps you can take and what tools you can use in order to put real-time conversations back at that center of marketing and sales, where they belong.

If you want to keep *this* conversation going, drop by Drift.com and say hello. A human (or a chatbot) will be there to greet you.

About the Authors

DAVID CANCEL is the co-founder and CEO of Drift, the world's leading conversational marketing and sales platform, named to the Forbes Cloud 100, LinkedIn's Top 50 Startups, and Entrepreneur's Top Company Cultures. He is also a serial entrepreneur, podcast host (Seeking Wisdom), angel investor, and advisor.

A five-time founder and two-time CEO, Cancel was the founder and CTO of Compete.com (acquired by WPP), the founder and owner of Ghostery (acquired by Evidon), and the co-founder and CEO of Performable (acquired by HubSpot). After the acquisition of Performable, Cancel became the chief product officer at HubSpot, where he grew the product team from 20 to more than 100 engineers. Cancel has been featured by media outlets, including *The New York Times, Forbes, Fortune, Wired,* and *Fast Company,* and has guest lectured on entrepreneurship at Harvard, Harvard Business School, MIT, MIT's Sloan School of Management, and Bentley. In 2017, Harvard Business School named Cancel an Entrepreneur in Residence at the School's Arthur Rock Center for Entrepreneurship.

Cancel's blog davidcancel.com has been read by more than a million entrepreneurs, while his Twitter account @dcancel has more than 60,000 followers and is considered a "must-follow" for entrepreneurs and executives. He is also a regular speaker at marketing and sales conferences, including SaaStr, SaaSFest, Converted, Revenue Summit, and HYPERGROWTH.

Dave Gerhardt is VP of Marketing at Drift and a passionate advocate of building brands around compelling stories that connect with customers. Since joining Drift in 2015 as employee #6, Dave has helped to create the category of conversational marketing and get 150,000+ businesses onboard with Drift, and Drift has been profiled in more than

100 publications, including *The New York Times, Forbes, Fortune, TechCrunch* and the *Harvard Business Review*; and won recognition in the Forbes Cloud 100, LinkedIn's Top 50 Startups, Entrepreneur's Top Company Cultures, the NVCA's SaaS Company of the Year and the Boston Business Journal's Best Places to Work. Dave has spearheaded the creation of Drift's annual HYPERGROWTH conference, which has grown to over 12,000 marketing and sales professionals to date. Dave is also the co-host of Seeking Wisdom, Drift's popular podcast that explores personal and professional growth.

Before joining Drift, Dave worked at some of the fastest-growing SaaS and B2B marketing companies in the Greater Boston Area, including HubSpot and Constant Contact.

Index

Page references followed by *fig* indicate an illustrated figure; followed by *t* indicate a table.

A